Just for **FUN**

Just

for FUN

THE STORY OF AN ACCIDENTAL REVOLUTIONARY

LINUS TORVALDS,

CREATOR OF **LINUX**,

AND DAVID DIAMOND

TEXERE

New York · London

Published by
TEXERE
55 East 52nd Street
New York, NY 10055

Tel: 212.317.5106
Fax: 212.317.5178
www.etexere.com

In the UK:
TEXERE Publishing Ltd.
71-77 Leadenhall Street
London, EC3A 3DE

Tel: 20 7204 3644
Fax: 20 7208 6701
www.etexere.co.uk

This publication is designed to provide accurate and authoritative information in regard to the subject manner covered. It is sold with the understanding that the publisher is not engaged in rendering legal, accounting, or other professional services. If legal advice or other expert assistance is required, the services or a competent professional person should be sought.

Library of Congress Cataloging-in-Publication Data has been applied for.

ISBN 1-58799-080-6

10 9 8 7 6 5 4 3 2 1

To Tove and Patricia, Daniela, and Celeste. I always wanted to be surrounded by young women, and you made it so.

To Tia and Kaley. Boy do I feel blessed.

This wouldn't qualify as acknowledgments without the dropping of some important names, so here goes:

We acknowledge our editor, Adrian Zackheim, who caved in to our every demand; Erin Richnow, the HarperCollins assistant editor who was more on top of this project than we were; our agents, Bill Gladstone of Waterside Productions and Kris Dahl of ICM, who couldn't have been speedier in the forwarding of our checks to us; Sara Torvalds, who has the best backup memory on the Fennoscandia peninsula—and operates in three languages—and William and Ruth Diamond, who read the original manuscript and kept repeating, "No, really, it's good."

My heart was in my throat when he was growing up: How on Earth was he going to meet any nice girls that way?

—Anna Torvalds

Introduction:
Post-its from a Revolution

During the euphoria of the final years of the twentieth century, a revolution was happening among all the other revolutions. Seemingly overnight, the Linux operating system caught the world's attention. It had exploded from the small bedroom of its creator, Linus Torvalds, to attract a cultish following of near-militant geeks. Suddenly it was infiltrating the corporate powerhouses controlling the planet. From a party of one it now counted millions of users on every continent, including Antarctica, and even outer space, if you count NASA outposts. Not only was it the most common operating system running server computers dishing out all the content on the World Wide Web, but its very development model—an intricate web of its own, encompassing hundreds of thousands of volunteer computer programmers—had grown to become the largest collaborative project in the history of the world. The open source philosophy behind it all was simple: Information, in this case the source code or basic instructions behind the operating system, should be free and freely shared for anyone interested in improving upon it. But those improvements should also be freely shared. The same concept had supported centuries of scientific discovery. Now it was finding a home in the corporate sphere, and it was possible to imagine its potential as a framework for creating the best of anything: a legal strategy, an opera.

Some folks caught a glimpse of the future and didn't like what they saw. Linus's round, bespectacled countenance became a favored dartboard target within Microsoft Corporation, which was now faced with its first honest-to-goodness competitive threat. But, more often, people wanted to learn more about the kid who—if he did not start it all—at least jump-started it and was, in effect, its leader. The trouble was, the more successful Linux and open source became, the less he wanted to talk about it. The accidental revolutionary started Linux because playing on a computer was fun (and also because the alternatives weren't that attractive). So when someone tried to convince him to speak at a major event by telling him that his millions of followers just wanted to at least see him, in the flesh, Linus good-naturedly offered to participate in a dunk-tank instead. That would be more fun, he explained. And a way of raising money. They declined. It wasn't their idea of how to run a revolution.

Revolutionaries aren't born. Revolutions can't be planned. Revolutions can't be managed.

Revolutions happen. . . .

—David Diamond

X-Authentication-Warning: penguin.transmeta.com:
  torvalds owned process doing-bs
Date: Mon, 18 Oct 1999 14:12:27-0700 (PDT)
From: Linus Torvalds <torvalds@transmeta.com>
To: David Diamond <ddiamond@well.com>
Subject:Ho humm..
MIME-Version: 1.0

I hope this is still your email address. I noticed
that I didn't have any contact information for you
anywhere, probably because I've trashed your business
card along with all the others, and because you've
actually contacted me by phone much more than by
email.

I've thought a lot over the weekend, and if you're
interested, I think I'm getting more and more interested. Let's cut a deal: If you think we can make a
fun book, and more importantly if you think we can
have fun making it, let's go for it. You'd drag me
(with family) camping and (without family) skydiving.
Things that I wouldn't ever do otherwise, just
because I think I'm too busy. Give me an excuse to do
the things I haven't done during the last three years
even though all the opportunities are there . . . So
maybe I wouldn't read a book about me when it's done,
but at least I'd have fun with it.

                                                Linus

. . . And sometimes, revolutionaries just get stuck with it.
                                        Linus Torvalds

Contents

Acknowledgments

The authors wish to acknowledge the following establishments for their role in creating this book—or at least making it fun. (None of these places have paid us any money. Which is a damn shame.)

FM 107.7 the Bone. Classic Rock That Rocks; Zelda's Restaurant, Capitola; Kiva Retreat House, Santa Cruz; Hagashi West Restaurant, Palo Alto; Malibu Grand Prix, Redwood Shores; Bodega Bay Lodge, Bodega Bay; Saturn Cafe, Santa Cruz; Cafe Marmalade, Ross; Half Moon Bay Boardshop, Half Moon Bay; Santa Cruz Billiards, Santa Cruz; Café Reyes, Point Reyes Station; California Sushi and Grill, San Jose; Santa Clara Golf and Tennis Club, Santa Clara; Ideal Bar and Grill, Santa Cruz; Silver Peso Bar ("Where Janis Played"), Larkspur; Rosie McCann's Irish Pub and Restaurant, Santa Cruz; Mayflower Inn, San Rafael; Grover Hot Springs State Park, Markleeville; Left Bank Restaurant, Larkspur; Potrero Brewing Company, San Francisco; The Rice Table, San Rafael; Ross Valley Swim and Tennis Club, Kentfield; Fallen Leaf Lake Marina, Fallen Leaf Lake; Peet's Coffee and Tea, Greenbrae; Hawthorne Lane Restaurant, San Francisco; Indian Springs Resort, Calistoga; Samurai Sushi, Sausalito; Blowfish Sushi, San Francisco; Paramount's Great America, Santa Clara; Robata Grill Sushi, Mill Valley; Buckeye Roadhouse, Mill Valley; Barnes and Noble, San Jose; Sushi Ran, Sausalito; 23 Ross Common, Ross; KFOG-104.5 FM; Rutherford Grill, Rutherford; In-N-Out Burger, Santa Rosa; Seto Sushi, Sunnyvale.

Preface:
The Meaning of Life I
(Sex, War, Linux)

SETTING: This book has its origins in a late-model black Ford Expedition in the southbound lanes of Interstate 5, somewhere in California's Central Valley. Linus and Tove Torvalds and their young daughters, Patricia and Daniela, are accompanied by an interloper as they travel 351 miles to Los Angeles, where they will visit the zoo and an IKEA outlet.

DAVID: Now I've got a fundamental question to think about, and it's sort of important. What do you want to get across in this book?

LINUS: Well, I want to explain the meaning of life.

TOVE: Linus, did you remember to fill the gas tank?

L: I have a theory about the meaning of life. We can, in the first chapter, explain to people what the meaning of life is. We get them hooked that way. Once they're hooked and pay for the book, we can just fill up the rest with random crap.

D: Oh yes. That sounds like a plan. Someone told me that since the dawn of man there have been two lingering questions. *One:* "What is the meaning of life?" and *Two:* "What can I do with all this pocket change that accumulates at the end of the day?"

L: I have the answer to the first one.

D: *What's* the answer to the first one?

L: Basically it is short and sweet. It won't give your life any meaning, but it tells you what's going to happen. There are three things that have meaning for life. They are the motivational factors for everything in your life—for anything that *you* do or any living thing does: The first is survival, the second is social order, and the third is entertainment. Everything in life progresses in that order. And there is nothing after entertainment. So, in a sense, the implication is that the meaning of life is to reach that third stage. And once you've reached the third stage, you're done. But you have to go through the other stages first.

D: You're going to have to explain this a little more.

PATRICIA: Papa, can we stop for chocolate ice cream? I would like to have some chocolate ice cream now!

T: No, sweetie. You have to wait. When we stop to go potty you can have ice cream.

L: I'll give you a few examples so you can kind of get the idea. And the obvious one is sex. It started out as survival, but it became a social thing. That's why you get married. And then it becomes entertainment.

P: Then I have to go potty.

D: How is it entertaining?

L: Okay, I'm talking to the wrong person. How about this one?

D: No, go back to sex.

L: It's also on another level . . .

D: (to self): Oh, entertaining to participate in as opposed to watch. Okay, I get it.

L: . . . On another level, if you look at the illusion of sex in a biological sense—How did sex come about in the first place? It was survival. It wasn't entertaining initially. It was just getting together. Okay, let's drop the sex part.

D: No, no. I think this is a whole chapter.

L: Let's pick war instead. It's obvious it started as survival, because there's a big guy between you and the water hole. Next, you need to fight the guy for a wife. And then war becomes a social-order thing. That's how it was long before the Middle Ages.

D: War as a means of establishing social order.

L: Right. And also a means of establishing yourself as part of the social order. Nobody cares about social order, per se. Everybody cares about his own place in that order. It's the same thing whether you're a hen in a pecking order or you're a human.

D: And now war is for entertainment?

L: That's right.

D: Maybe for people watching it on TV. For them it might be entertaining.

L: Computer games. War games. CNN. Well, the *reason* for war can often be entertaining. But also the perception of war is entertaining. And the reason for sex is often entertaining. Sure, the survival part is still there, especially if you're Catholic, right? But even if you're Catholic, sometimes you probably think about the entertainment part, too. So it doesn't have to be plain entertainment. In everything, a piece of the motivation might be survival, a piece might be social order, and the rest might be entertainment. Okay, look at technology. Technology came about as survival. And survival is not about just surviving, it's about surviving better. You get a windmill that draws water from the well . . .

D: Or fire.

L: Right. It's still survival, but it hasn't progressed to social order and entertainment.

D: Now how has technology progressed to social order?

L: Well, actually most of industrialization has been really just survival, or surviving better. In cars, that meant making faster cars and nicer cars. But then you get to technology in a social sense. That brings us the telephone. And TV, to some degree. A lot of the early TV stuff was basically for indoctrination. Radio, too. That's why countries often started investing in radio, for the social-order side of it.

D: Establishing and maintaining social order . . .

L: Right, but then it just goes past that. Today, TV is obviously used mostly for entertainment. And right now you see all these wireless mobile phones. It's basically social. But it's moving into entertainment, too.

D: So what's the future of technology? We've gone beyond the survival stage and now we're in the social stage, right?

L: Right. All technology used to do was make life easier. It was all about getting places faster, buying things cheaper, having better houses, whatever. So what's so different about information technology? What comes after the fact that everybody is connected? What more is there to do? Sure, you can connect better, but that's not fundamentally different. So where is technology taking us? In my opinion, the next big step is entertainment.

D: Everything eventually evolves into entertainment . . .

L: But this also explains why Linux is so successful, to some degree. Think of the three motivational factors. First is survival, which people with computers take for granted. Quite frankly, if you have a computer, you've already bought your food and stuff like that. The second is for social order, and the social side is certainly motivational for geeks sitting inside their own cubicles.

D: You said something really smart at Comdex, something about Linux development being a global team sport. So, you basically made that happen, dude.

L: Linux is a great example of why people love team sports, and especially being part of a team.

D: Yeah, sitting in front of a computer all day, you'd probably want to feel like you were part of something. Anything.

L: It's social, like any other team sport. Imagine people on a football team, especially in high school. The social part of Linux is really, really important. But Linux is also entertainment, the kind of entertainment that is very hard to buy with money. Money is a very powerful motivational factor when you're at the level of survival, because it's easy to buy survival. It's very easy to barter for those kinds of things. But suddenly when you're at the level of entertainment, money . . .

D: Money is useless?

L: No, it's not useless, because obviously you can buy movies, fast cars, vacations. There are a lot of things you can buy that can help make your situation better.

T: Linus, we need to change Daniela. And Patricia has to go potty. I need a cappuccino. Do you think we can find a Starbucks here? Where are we?

D: (looks up): Based on the odor, I think we're near King City.

L: Now all this is on a bigger scale. It's not just about people, it's about life. It's like the Law of Entropy. In this Entropy Law of Life, everything moves from survival to entertainment, but that doesn't mean that on a local scale it can't go backward, and obviously it essentially does. Things just disintegrate sometimes.

D: But as a system, everything is moving in the same direction . . .

L: Everything is moving in the same direction, but not at the same time. So basically sex has reached entertainment, war is close to it, technology is pretty much there. The new things are things that are just survival. Like, hopefully, space travel will at some point be an issue of survival, then it will be social, then entertainment. Look at civilization as a cult. I mean, that also follows the same pattern. Civilization starts as survival. You get together to survive better and you build up your social structure.

Then eventually civilization exists purely for entertainment. Okay, well, not purely. And it doesn't have to be bad entertainment. The ancient Greeks are known for having had a very strong social order, and they also had a lot of entertainment. They're known for having had the best philosophers of their time.

D: Okay, so how does this tie in to the meaning of life?

L: It doesn't really. It just says that . . . that's kind of the problem here.

D: This is the little link you're going to have to think about.

P: Mama, look at the cows.

L: So, if you know that life is all about this progression, then obviously your purpose in life is to make this progression. And the progression is not one single progression. Everything you do is part of many progressions. It can also be, "What can I do to make society better?" You know that you're a part of society. You know that society is moving in this direction. You can help society move in this direction.

T: (holding nose): It smells horrible here.

L: So what this builds up to is that in the end we're all here to have fun. We might as well sit down and relax, and enjoy the ride.

D: Just for fun?

Birth of a NERD

I.

I was an ugly child.

What can I say? I hope some day Hollywood makes a film about Linux, and they'll be sure to cast somebody who looks like Tom Cruise in the lead role—but in the non-Hollywood version, things don't work out that way.

Don't get me wrong. It's not as if I looked like the Hunchback of Notre Dame. Envision instead large front teeth, so that anybody seeing a picture of me in my younger years gets a slightly beaverish impression. Imagine also a complete lack of taste in clothes, coupled with the traditional oversized Torvalds nose, and the picture starts to complete in your mind.

The nose, I'm sometimes told, is "stately." And people—well, at least in our family—say that the size of a man's nose is indicative of other things, too. But tell that to a boy in his teens, and he won't much care. To him, the nose only serves to overshadow the teeth. The picture of the profiles of three generations of Torvalds men is just a painful reminder that yes, there is more nose than man there. Or so it seems at the time.

Now, to add to the picture, start filling in the details. Brown hair (what here in the United States is called blond, but in Scandinavia is just "brown"), blue eyes, and a slight shortsightedness that makes wearing glasses a good idea. And, as wearing them possibly takes attention away from the nose, wear them I do. All the time.

Oh, and I already mentioned the atrocious taste in clothes. Blue is the color of choice, so that usually means blue jeans with a blue turtleneck. Or maybe turquoise. Whatever. Happily, our family wasn't very much into photography. That way there's less incriminating evidence.

There are a few photographs. In one of them I'm around thirteen years old, posing with my sister Sara, who is sixteen months younger. She looks fine. But I'm a gangly vision, a skinny pale kid contorting for the photographer, who was probably my mother. She most likely snapped the little gem on her way out the door to her job as an editor at the Finnish News Agency.

Being born at the very end of the year, on the 28th of December, meant that I was pretty much the youngest in my class at school. And that in turn meant the smallest. Later on, being half a year younger than most of your classmates doesn't matter. But it certainly does during the first few years of school.

And do you know what? Surprisingly, none of it really matters all that much. Being a beaverish runt with glasses, bad hair days most of the time (and *really* bad hair days the rest of the time), and bad clothes doesn't really matter. Because I had a charming personality.

Not.

No, let's face it, I was a nerd. A geek. From fairly early on. I didn't duct-tape my glasses together, but I might as well have, because I had all the other traits. Good at math, good at physics, and with no social graces whatsoever. And this was before being a nerd was considered a good thing.

Everybody has probably known someone in school like me. The boy who is known as being best at math—not because he studies hard, but just because he is. I was that person in my class.

But let me fill in the picture some more, before you start feeling too sorry for me. A nerd I may have been, and a runt, but I did okay. I wasn't exactly athletic, but I wasn't a hopeless klutz either. The game of choice during breaks at school was "brännboll"— a game of skill and speed in which two teams try to decimate each other by throwing a ball around. And while I wasn't ever the top player, I was usually picked fairly early on.

So in the social rankings I might have been a nerd, but, on the whole, school was good. I got good grades without having to work at it—never truly great grades, exactly because I *didn't* work at it. And an accepted place in the social order. Nobody else really seemed to care too much about my nose; this was almost certainly, in retrospect, because they cared about their own problems a whole lot more.

Looking back, I realize that most other children seem to have had pretty bad taste in clothes, too. We grow up and suddenly somebody else makes that particular decision. In my case, it's the marketing staffs for high-tech companies, the people who select the T-shirts and jackets that will be given away free at conferences. These days, I dress pretty much exclusively in vendorware, so I never have to pick out clothes. And I have a wife to make the decisions that complete my wardrobe, to pick out things like sandals and socks. So I never have to worry about it again.

And I've grown into my nose. At least for now, I'm more man than nose.

II.

It probably won't surprise anyone that some of my earliest and happiest memories involve playing with my grandfather's old electronic calculator.

This was my mother's father, Leo Waldemar Törnqvist, who was a professor of statistics at Helsinki University. I remember having tons of fun calculating the sine of various random numbers. Not because I actually cared all that much for the answer (after all, not many people do), but because this was a long time ago, and calculators didn't just give you the answer. They *calculated* it. And they blinked a lot while doing so, mainly in order to give you some feedback that "Yes, I'm still alive, and it takes me ten seconds to do this calculation, and in the meantime I'll blink for you to show how much work I do."

That was fascinating. Much more exciting than a modern calculator that won't even break into a sweat when doing something as simple as calculating a plain sine of a number. With those early devices you knew that what they did was *hard*. They made it very clear indeed.

I don't actually remember the first time I saw a computer, but I must have been around eleven at the time. It was probably in 1981, when my grandfather bought a new Commodore VIC-20. Since I had spent so much time playing with his magic calculator, I must have been thrilled—panting with excitement to start playing with the new computer—but I can't really seem to remember that. In fact, I don't even remember when I got really into computers at all. It started slowly, and it grew on me.

The VIC-20 was one of the first ready-made computers meant for the home. It required no assembly. You just plugged it into the TV and turned it on, and there it sat, with a big all-caps "READY" at the top of the screen and a big blinking cursor just waiting for you to do something.

The big problem was that there really wasn't that much to do on the thing. Especially early on, when the infrastructure for commercial programs hadn't yet started to materialize. The only thing you could really do was to program it in BASIC. Which was exactly what my grandfather started doing.

Now, my grandfather saw this new toy mainly *as* a toy, but also as a glorified calculator. Not only could it compute the sine of a number a lot faster than the old electronic calculator, but you could tell it to do this over and over automatically. He also could now do at home many of the things he had done with the big computers at the university.

And he wanted me to share in the experience. He also was trying to get me interested in math.

So I would sit on his lap and he would have me type in his programs, which he had carefully written out on paper because he wasn't comfortable with computers. I don't know how many other preteen boys sat in their grandfather's room, being taught how to simplify arithmetic expressions and type them correctly into a computer, but I remember doing that. I don't remember what the calculations were all about, and I don't think I had a single clue about what I really did when I did it, but I was there, helping him. It probably took us much longer than it would have taken him alone, but who knows? I grew comfortable with the keyboard, something my grandfather never did. I would do this after school, or whenever my mother dropped me off at my grandparents' apartment.

And I started reading the manuals for the computer, typing in the example programs. There were examples of simple games that you could program yourself. If you did it right you wound up with a guy that walked across the screen, in bad graphics, and then you could change it and make the guy walk across the screen in different colors. You could just *do* that.

It's the greatest feeling.

I started writing my own. The first program I wrote was the first program everybody else starts out with:

```
10 PRINT "HELLO"
20 GOTO 10
```

This does exactly what you expect it to do. It prints out HELLO on the screen. Forever. Or at least until you kill it out of boredom.

But it's the first step. Some people stop there. To them, it's a stupid exercise because why would you want to print out HELLO a million times? But it was invariably the first example in the manuals that came with those early home computers.

And the magic thing is that you can change it. My sister tells me that I made a radical second version of this program that didn't just write out HELLO, but instead wrote SARA IS THE BEST on the screen, over and over again. Ordinarily I wasn't such a loving older brother. Apparently the gesture made a big impression on her.

I don't remember doing it. As soon as I wrote a program I would forget about it and move on to the next one.

III.

Let me tell you about Finland. Sometime in October the skies turn an unpleasant shade of gray, and it always looks as if it will either rain or snow. You wake up every day to this gloominess of anticipation. The rain will be chilly and it will rinse away any evidence of summer. When the snow comes, it has that magical quality of making everything bright and painting the place with a veneer of optimism. The trouble is, the optimism lasts about three days but the snow remains for month after bone-numbingly cold month.

By January you sort of wander around in a shadowy daze, if you choose to go outside. It's a season of moist, bulky clothes and slipping on the ice hockey rink they created by hosing down the grammar school field you traverse as a short-cut to the bus. On Helsinki streets it means dodging the occasional tottering matron who was probably somebody's gracious grandmother back in September but by 11 A.M. on a Tuesday in January is weaving on the sidewalks from her vodka breakfast. Who can blame her? It will be dark again in a few hours, and there isn't a lot to do. But there was an indoor sport that got me through the winter: programming.

Morfar (the Swedish word for "Mother's Father") would be there much of the time, but not all the time. He doesn't mind if you sit in his room when he's away. You beg up the money for your first computer book. Everything is in English and it is necessary to decode the language. It's difficult to understand technical literature in a language you don't really know that well. You use your allowance to buy computer magazines. One of them contains a program for Morse code. The odd thing about this particular program is that it's not written in the BASIC language. Instead, it's written as a list of numbers that could be translated by hand to machine language—the zeros and ones that the computer reads.

That's how you discover that the computer doesn't really speak BASIC. Instead it operates according to a much more simple language. Helsinki kids are playing hockey and skiing with their parents in the woods. You're learning how a computer actually works. Unaware that programs exist to translate human-readable numbers into the zeros and ones that a computer understands, you just start writing programs in number form and do the conversions by hand. This is programming in machine language, and by doing it you start to do things you wouldn't have thought possible before. You are able to push what the computer can do. You control every single small detail. You start to think about how you can do things slightly faster in a smaller space. Since there's no abstraction layer between you and the computer, you get fairly close. This is what it's like to be intimate with a machine.

You're twelve, thirteen, fourteen, whatever. Other kids are out playing soccer. Your grandfather's computer is more interesting. His machine is its own world, where logic rules. There are maybe three people in class with computers and only one of them uses it for the same reasons. You hold weekly meetings. It's the only social activity on the calendar, except for the occasional computer sleepover.

And you don't mind. This is fun.

This is after the divorce. Dad lives in another part of Helsinki. He thinks his kid should have more than one interest, so he signs you up for basketball, his favorite sport. This is a disaster. You're the runt of the team. After a season and a half, you use all sorts of nasty language to tell him you're quitting, that basketball is *his* sport, not yours. Your new half-brother, Leo, will be more athletic. Then, too, he will eventually become Lutheran, like 90 percent of the Finnish population. That's when Dad, the staunch agnostic, realized he might be a failure as a parent—something he suspected years earlier, when Sara joined the Catholic church.

The grandfather with the computer isn't really a jolly sort. He's balding, slightly overweight. He literally is something of an absent-minded professor and kind of hard to approach. He's just not an extrovert. Picture a mathematician who would stare out into space and not say anything while he was thinking about something. You could never tell what he was thinking about. Complexity analysis? Mrs. Sammalkorpi down the hall? I'm the same way—famous for zoning out. When I'm sitting in front of the computer, I get really upset and irritable if somebody disturbs me. Tove could elaborate on this point.

My most vivid memories of Morfar take place not at his computer but at his little red cottage. In Helsinki it used to be common for people to keep a small summer place consisting of maybe a single thirty-foot by thirty-foot room. The little houses are on a tiny plot of land, maybe 150 square feet, and people go there to tinker in their gardens. They typically have an apartment in the city and then this little place to grow potatoes or tend a few apple trees or cultivate roses. It's usually older people because younger ones are busy working. These people get ridiculously competitive about whatever it is they are growing. That's where Morfar planted my apple tree, a small sapling. Maybe it's still there, unless it became so abundant that an envious neighbor snuck onto his property during the brief summer darkness and chopped it down.

Four years after introducing me to computers, Morfar develops a blood clot in his brain and becomes paralyzed on one side. It's a shock to everyone. He's in the hospital for about a year and he's the closest family you have, but it doesn't affect you that much. Maybe it's defensive or maybe it's just because you're so insensitive when you're young. He is absolutely not the same person anymore and you don't like going to see him. You go maybe every two weeks. Your mother goes more often. So does your sister, who early on assumed the role of the family social worker.

After he dies, the machine comes to live with you. There isn't any real discussion about it.

IV.

Let's step back for a moment.

Finland might be the hippest country on Earth right now, but centuries ago, it was little more than a stopover for Vikings as they "traded" with Constantinople. Later, when the neighboring Swedes wanted to pacify the Finns, they sent in English-born Bishop Henry, who arrived in the year 1155 on a mission for the Catholic church. Those proselytizing Swedes manned the Finnish fortresses to ward off the Russians, and eventually won against the empire to our East in the struggle for control. To spur population of the Finnish colony in the following centuries, Swedes were offered land and tax incentives. Swedes ran the show until 1714, when Russia took over for a seven-year interlude. Then Sweden won back its colony until 1809, when Russia and Napoleon attacked Finland; it remained under Russian control until the Communist Revolution in 1917. Meanwhile, the descendants of the early Swedish immigrants are the 350,000 Swedish speakers in Finland today, a group that represents about five percent of the population.

Including my wacky family.

My maternal great-grandfather was a relatively poor farmer from Jappo, a small town near the city of Vasa. He had six sons, at least two of whom earned Ph.D.'s. That says a lot about the prospects for advancement in Finland. Yes, you get sick of the winter darkness and taking off your shoes upon entering a house. But you can get a university education for free. It's a far cry from what happens in the United States, where so many kids grow up with a sense of hopelessness. One of those six sons was my grandfather, Leo Waldemar Törnqvist, the fellow who introduced me to computing.

Then there was my paternal grandfather. He was the fellow who concocted the name Torvalds, fashioning it out of his middle name. He was named Ole Torvald Elis Saxberg. My grandfather had been born fatherless (Saxberg was his mother's maiden name) and was given the last name Karanko by the gentleman my great-grandmother eventually married. Farfar ("Father's father") didn't like the guy, enough so he changed his name. He dropped the last name and added an "s" to Torvald on the theory that this made it sound more substantial. Torvald on its own means "Thor's domain." He should have started from scratch, because what the adding of an "s" does is destroy the meaning of the root name, and confuse both Swedish-and Finnish-speaking people, who don't know how the heck to pronounce it. And they think it should be spelled Thorwalds. There are twenty-one Torvalds in the world, and we're all related. We all endure the confusion.

Maybe that's why I'm always just "Linus" on the Net. "Torvalds" is just too confusing.

This grandfather didn't teach at a university. He was a journalist and poet. His first job was as editor-in-chief of a small-town newspaper about 100 kilometers west of Helsinki. He got sacked for drinking on the job with a little too much regularity. His marriage to my grandmother broke down. He moved to the city of Turku in Southwestern Finland, where he remarried and finally became editor-in-chief of the newspaper and published several books of poetry, although he always struggled with a drinking problem. We would visit him there for Christmas and Easter, and to see my grandmother, too. Farmor Märta lives in Helsinki, where she is known for making killer pancakes.

Farfar died five years ago.

Okay: I've never read any of his books. It's a fact that my father points out to total strangers.

Journalists are everywhere in my family. Legend has it that

one of my great-grandfathers, Ernst von Wendt, was a journalist and novelist who was on the White side and arrested by the Reds during the Finnish Civil War that followed our independence from Russia in 1917. (Okay. I never read his books, either, and am told I'm not missing much.) My father, Nils (known to everyone as Nicke), is a television and radio journalist who was active in the Communist Party since he was a college student in the 1960s. He developed his political leanings when he learned about some of the atrocities committed against communist sympathizers in Finland. Decades later he admits that his enthusiasm for communism may have been born out of naiveté. He met my mother Anna (known as Mikke) when they were both rebellious university students in the 1960s. His story is that they were on an outing for a club of Swedish-speaking students, of which he was president. He had a rival for my mother's attention, and as they were preparing for the return bus trip to Helsinki, he instructed the rival to oversee the loading of the bus. He used the occasion to grab the seat next to my mother and convince her to go out with him. (And people call *me* the family genius!)

I was born more or less between campus protests, probably with something like Joni Mitchell playing in the background. Our family love nest was a room in my grandparents' apartment. A laundry basket served as my first crib. Thankfully, that period isn't easy to remember. Sometime around my three-month birthday, Papa signed up for his required eleven-month Army service rather than go to jail as the conscientious objector he probably was. He became such a good soldier and such an excellent marksman that he was rewarded with frequent weekend leave privileges. The family tale is that my sister Sara was conceived during one of those conjugal visits. When my mother wasn't juggling two blond-haired rugrats, she worked as an editor on the foreign desk at the Finnish News Agency. Today she works as a graphics editor.

It's all part of the journalism mini-dynasty that I miraculously escaped. Sara has her own business translating reports for the news, and she also works at the Finnish News Agency. My half-brother, Leo Torvalds, is a video-type person who wants to direct films. Because my family members are basically all journalists, I feel qualified to joke with reporters about knowing what scum they are. I'm aware that I come off as a complete jerk when I say that, but over the years our home in Finland hosted its share of reporters who stopped at nothing to get their story, or who made up their stories from scratch, or who always seemed to have had just a little too much to drink. Okay: a lot too much to drink.

That's when it would be time to hide out in the bedroom. Or maybe Mom is having an emotional rough spot. We live in a two-bedroom apartment on the second floor of an unremarkable pale yellow building on Stora Robertsgatan, in Rödbergen, a small area near the center of Helsinki. Sara and her obnoxious sixteen-month-older brother share a bedroom. There's a small park nearby, named after the Sinebrychoff family, which owns a local brewery. That has always struck me as being odd, but is it any different from naming a basketball stadium after an office products vendor? (Because a cat had once been seen there, Sinebrychoffsparken was henceforth known in my family as the "Catpark.") There's a vacant little house there in which pigeons would gather. The park is built on a hill, and in the winter it's a place to sled. Another play area is the cement courtyard behind our building, or on the building itself. Whenever we play hide-and-seek, it's fun to climb the ladder five stories up to the roof.

But no fun could compare to computer fun. With the computer at home, it was possible to stay up all night with it. Every boy stays up "reading" *Playboy* under the bedcovers. But instead of reading *Playboy* I would fake sleeping, wait for Mom to go away, jump up and sit in front of the computer. This was before the era of chatrooms.

"Linus, it's food time!" Some of the time you don't even come out. Then your mother starts telling her journalist friends that you are such a low-maintenance child that all she has to do to keep you happy is store you in a dark closet with a computer and occasionally throw in some dry pasta. She's not far off the mark. Nobody

was worried about this kid getting kidnapped. (Hmmm. Would anybody have noticed?) Computers were actually better for kids when they were less sophisticated, when dweebie youngsters like me could tinker under the hood. These days, computers suffer from the same problem as cars: As they became more complex, they became more difficult for people to take apart and put back together, and, as a result, learn what they are all about. When was the last time you did anything on your car more involved than changing the oil filter?

Instead of tinkering under the metaphoric hoods of their computers, kids these days are playing too many games, and losing their minds. Not that there's anything wrong with games. They were some of my earliest programs.

There was one in which you were controlling a small submarine in a grotto. It's a very standard game concept. The world moves sideways, pans, and as a player you're the submarine and you have to avoid hitting the walls and monster fish. The only thing that actually moves is the world. The fish move with the world. It all starts moving faster and faster the longer you play. Meanwhile, the grotto gets smaller and smaller. You cannot win this game, but that was never the point. It's fun to play for a week or so and go on to the next game. The whole point is just writing the code to make it all happen.

There are other toys, like model planes and ships and cars and railroads. At one point, Dad buys expensive German model trains. The reasoning is that he never had a model train set as a kid, and that it would be a good father-son hobby. It's fun, but it doesn't come close to the challenge of computers. The only time your computer privileges are taken away is not for spending too much time on the machine but as punishment for something else, like fighting with Sara. Throughout grammar school and high school the two of you are extremely competitive, particularly when it comes to academics.

All the competition yields some good results. Without my constant taunting, Sara never would have been motivated to upstage me by writing six final essays, instead of the five required to graduate from high school in Finland. On the other hand, Sara is to be thanked for the fact that my English is not atrocious. She always made fun of my English, which for years was typical Finnish-English. That's why it improved. For that matter, my mother teased me, too—but mostly about the fact that I was showing little interest in the female schoolmates who wanted to be tutored by the "Math Genius."

At times we lived with my dad and his girlfriend, at other times Sara lived with my dad and I lived with my mom. At times both of us lived with my mom. By the way, the Swedish language has no equivalent to the term "dysfunctional family." As a result of the divorce, we didn't have a lot of money. One of my most distinct memories is of the times when my Mom would have to pawn her only investment—the single share of stock in the Helsinki telephone company, that you owned as part of having a telephone. It was probably worth about $500, and every so often, when things got particularly tight, she would have to take the certificate to a pawn shop. I remember going with her once and feeling embarrassed about it. (Now I'm on the board of directors of the same company. In fact, the Helsinki Telephone Company is the only company where I'm a board member.) Embarrassed was also how I felt when, after I had saved most of the money for my first watch, Mom wanted me to ask my grandfather for the money to pay for the rest.

There was a period when my mother was working nights, so Sara and I had to fend for ourselves in getting dinner. We were supposed to go to the corner store and buy food on our charge account. Instead, we would buy candy and it would be wonderful to stay up late on the computer. Under such circumstances, other boys would have been "reading" *Playboy* above the covers.

Shortly after my grandfather had his stroke, Mormor didn't feel like taking care of herself. She was bedridden in a nursing home for ten years with what she called "wooziness." When she had been in the hospital for a couple of years, we moved into her apartment. It was on the first floor of a solid old Russian-era building on Petersgatan, near the gracious park that lines Helsinki's waterfront. There was a small kitchen and three bedrooms. Sara got the big bedroom. The gangly teenager, who was happy with a dark closet and periodic dry pasta, moved into the smallest one. I hung thick black drapes on the windows so no sunlight would seep in. The computer found a home on a tiny desk against the window, maybe two feet from my bed.

I was vaguely aware of Linus Torvalds when an editor of the San Jose Mercury News *Sunday magazine asked me to write a profile of him in the spring of 1999. Linux had become something of a buzzword the previous spring, when a succession of companies starting with Netscape had adopted either the notion of open source code or the operating system itself. Not that I had been up on the developments. In the early 1990s I had edited a magazine that dealt with Unix and Open Source issues, so there was a dusty reference sentence floating in my brain. In that reference, Linus was a Finnish college student who wrote a powerful version of Unix in his dorm room and distributed it freely over the Internet. It was not quite an accurate reference. The editor phoned because Linus had just been the star attraction—and mobbed—at a recent Linux show in San Jose, which prompted the editor to lure me into the assignment with the words, "We've got a global superstar right here in, uh, Santa Clara." He faxed over some newspaper reports.*

Linus had moved to Silicon Valley two years earlier and was working for the then-secretive Transmeta Corporation, which had for years been developing a microprocessor that promised to upend the computer industry. He somehow had a job that allowed him to maintain his time-consuming position as the ultimate leader of Linux and final authority on any changes made to the operating system. (His followers had, in fact, initiated the legal maneuvering that gave him legal ownership of the Linux trademark.) And he had time to trot the globe as poster boy for the burgeoning open source movement.

But he had become something of a mysterious folk hero. While

Bill Gates, everybody's favorite nemesis, was living in splendor in his Xanadu, Linus resided with his wife and toddler daughters in a cramped Santa Clara duplex. He apparently was unconcerned about the fabulous wealth that was being rained upon the flocks of less-talented programmers. And his very presence raised an unutterable conundrum among the stock-option-driven minions in Silicon Valley: How could anyone so brilliant possibly be so uninterested in getting rich?

Linus has no handlers, doesn't listen to voice mail, and rarely responds to email. It took weeks for me to get him on the phone, but once I did he easily agreed to an interview at his earliest convenience, which was about a month later: May 1999. Having developed a professional passion for putting interview subjects into compromising positions, I decided that a Finnish sauna might be the perfect backdrop for the profile. In a rented Mustang convertible, with a photographer at the wheel, we headed over to Santa Cruz and what was recommended as the Bay Area's best sauna, which was on the grounds of a New Age/nudist retreat.

He was armed with an opened can of Coke as he emerged from the innards of Transmeta's offices in an anonymous Santa Clara office park. He wore the programmer's uniform of jeans, conference T-shirt, and the inevitable socks-and-sandals combo that he claimed to have favored even before ever meeting another programmer. "It must be some programmer's law of nature," he reasoned when I asked about the footware choice.

The first question to Linus, as we sat in the backseat, was a throwaway. "Are your folks in technology?" I asked while fiddling with my tape recorder.

"No, they're all basically journalists," he replied, adding: "So I know what scum you are."

He didn't think he could get away with that.

"Oh. You come from scum?" I responded.

The world's best programmer laughed so hard that he coughed out a spray of Coke onto the back of the photographer-driver's neck. He turned red. This would be the start of a memorable afternoon.

It only got more bizarre. Finns are fanatical about their saunas and this was to be his first visit to one in nearly three years. The pale, naked superstar with steamed-up glasses sat on the highest perch, with his

wet tan hair matted down on his face and a river of sweat flowing down
what I would later, purely out of good will, describe as his "incipient
paunch." He was surrounded by tanned, self-obsessed Santa Cruzans and
their monotonous New Age rantings, and he seemed above it all, eagerly
pointing out the authentic features of the sauna. He had this beatific grin
on his face.

It's my conviction that, for the most part, people in Silicon Valley
are happier than everybody else. For one thing, they're at the control
panel of the economic revolution. More importantly, they're all getting
insufferably rich, both New Valley and Old Valley. But one never sees
people smile there, at least not outside the confines of their brokers' offices.

Most acclaimed technologists—even most of the unacclaimed
ones—have this immediate desire to let you know how brilliant they are.
And that they are critical players in a mission that is far more important
than, say, the struggle for world peace. That wasn't the case with Linus.
In fact, his lack of ego seemed downright disarming, and made him
uniquely likable amid Silicon Valley's bombastic elite. Linus appeared to
be above it all. Above the New Agers. Above the high-tech billionaires.
He seemed less like a reindeer caught in the global headlights than a
delightful alien beamed down to show us the madness of our selfish ways.

And I got the feeling that he didn't get out much.

Linus had earlier mentioned that an important part of the sauna
ritual involved sitting around afterward, drinking beer and discussing
world affairs. In preparation, we had stashed cans of Fosters in some
bushes. We retrieved the beers and settled into the "quiet" hot tub, where
we opened the Fosters while the photographer took his pictures. I found
Linus to be unexpectedly knowledgeable about American business history
and world politics. In his view, the United States would be better served
if both corporations and political parties adopted the conciliatory approach
of European politicians. He dipped his glasses into the hot tub in order
to clean them, mentioning that he really didn't need glasses but started
wearing them as an adolescent under the logic that they made his nose look
smaller. That's when a clothed female manager appeared at the hot tub
and humorlessly ordered us to hand over our beers, which were considered
contraband in the otherwise free-spirited surroundings.

Our only option was to shower, dress, and find a café for finishing the conversation. Most folks one meets in Silicon Valley have a cult-like zeal about them. They focus so intently on their business or killer application or The Industry that nothing else seems to exist. Nothing interrupts the continuous loop of self-congratulation that passes for conversation. But there we were, sitting in the sun at a microbrewery, sampling the Godawful barleywine, with Linus chattering away like an uncaged canary—confessing his addiction to Classic Rock and Dean Koontz, revealing his weakness for the dumbest sitcoms, sharing off-the-record family secrets.

And he didn't have any great desire to circulate among the rich and powerful. I asked him what he would like to say to Bill Gates, but he wasn't the least bit interested in even meeting the guy. "There wouldn't be much of a connection point," he reasoned. "I'm completely uninterested in the thing that he's the best in the world at. And he's not interested in the thing that maybe I'm the best in the world at. I couldn't give him advice in business and he couldn't give me advice in technology."

On the ride back over the mountain to Santa Clara, a black Jeep Cherokee pulled up alongside our car and its passenger yelled "Hey Linus!" and pulled out a throwaway camera to capture his apparent hero, who was sitting in the Mustang convertible's backseat, grinning in the breeze.

I showed up at his house a week later at bathtime. He fished his one-year-old blond daughter out of the tub and needed someplace to deposit her while he fished out his two-year-old blond daughter. He handed the younger daughter to me and she promptly let out a yell. His wife Tove, who had been in another room the entire time, emerged to help. She is on the short side, pleasant, and bears a thistle tattoo on her ankle. Soon we were all reading Swedish and English bedtime books to the kids. Then we stood around in the garage, amid unpacked belongings, where the Torvalds discussed the impossibility of affording "a real house with a real back yard" in Silicon Valley. There was no bitterness about it.

And, magnificently, they didn't appear to see the irony.

Soon we were watching Jay Leno, with cans of Guinness. That's when I realized it made sense to do a book.

V.

And I basically sat in front of a computer for four years.

Okay, there was school: Norssen High, the most central of Helsinki's five Swedish-language high schools, and the one nearest my home. Math and physics were interesting, and therefore easy. But whenever a subject involved rote memorization, my enthusiasm for that subject was diminished. So history was boring when it meant worrying about the date of the Battle of Hastings, but got interesting when you discussed the economic factors affecting a country. The same thing went for geography. I mean, who really *cares* how many people are in Bangladesh? Well, it might matter to a lot of folks, come to think of it. But the point is, it was far easier for me not to daydream about my computer when we were learning about something more engaging than statistics, like the monsoons, for example, or the reasons for the monsoons.

Phys ed was another matter entirely. I'm probably not breaking any news by revealing that I wasn't the most athletic guy on the Fennoscandia peninsula. I was skinny then, too, believe it or not. Gymnastics was actually okay to participate in. But when we would have soccer or ice hockey, it would be time for me to skip class.

This showed up in my grades. In Finland you get graded on a scale of four to ten. So I would earn tens and some nines for math, physics, biology, and everything else—but sevens for phys ed. Once there was a six. I earned a six in woodworking, too. That wasn't my strong sport, either. Other guys have well-crafted napkin holders or stools as souvenirs of woodworking class. All I have are a few splinters still lodged in my thumb after all these years. This is where it should be mentioned that my father-in-law was the one who built the fine swing set in our backyard on which my daughters spend so many happy hours.

My high school wasn't one of those institutions for exceptionally smart or ambitious kids, which are common in most U.S. cities. Such schools are pretty much against how Finland works. Finnish schools don't separate out the good students—or the losers, for that matter. However, each school did have its specialty, a subject that was not required but that you couldn't get at any other school. In the case of Norssen High School, it was Latin. And Latin was fun. More fun than learning Finnish and English.

Too bad it's a dead language. I'd love to get together with a few buddies and tell jokes in Latin or maybe discuss operating-system design strategies.

It was also fun to spend time in the coffee shop near school. It was a hangout for certain people, basically those who weren't hiding behind the school smoking cigarettes. You would go there instead of phys ed, or you would go there if you had an hour break between classes, which sometimes happened.

The place had been a haven for geeks since the days of slide rules. Also, it was the only café that let students buy things on account. That meant you would place your order and they would keep a written list of everything you ate or drank, and then when you somehow got the money together you would pay for it. Knowing the Finnish mania for technology, it's probably all recorded in a database these days.

My order was always the same: a Coke and a doughnut.

So young and already such a health food nut.

Generally speaking, I was better in school than my sister, Sara, who was more sociable, easier to look at, nicer to people—and, I should add, has been hired to translate this book into Swedish. But she beat me in the end because she took exams in more subjects. My interests were narrower. I was known as the Math Guy.

In fact, the only time I brought girls home was when they wanted to be tutored. It didn't happen all that many times, and it was never my idea, but my father harbors fantasies that they were interested in more than math tutoring. (In his mind, somehow they had bought into his Stately Nose = Stately Man equation.) If they were looking for any math-guy action, they certainly didn't have a willing partner. I mean, I could never even figure out what they were referring to by "heavy petting." I had spent time taking care of a neighbor's fifteen-pound cat and couldn't figure out what the big deal was.

Yes, I was definitely a geek. No question about it. This is before geekdom became sexy. Well, I guess it's not really sexy but hipper. What you had was someone who was both a geek and shy—or is that redundant?

So I would be sitting in front of a computer and be perfectly happy.

For high school graduation in Finland, you wear a fluffy white hat with a black band. There's a ceremony in which they hand out diplomas, and when you come home all your relatives are there with lots of champagne, flowers, and cake. And there's also a party for the entire class at a local restaurant. We did all that, and I guess I had fun, but I don't remember anything special about it. But ask me about the specs on my 68008-chip machine and I can rattle them off with total recall.

VI.

My first year at university was actually quite productive. I managed to earn the number of credits—which are called "study weeks" in the Finnish system—that one is supposed to earn. It was the only year that happened. Maybe it was the excitement of the new environment, or the opportunity to delve deeply into the topics, or because it was more comfortable for me to study than to become a social animal and puke on my friends with ritualistic regularity. I don't know what to blame for my adequate performance in that first year. But rest assured, it didn't happen again. My academic career took a sharp nosedive.

At that point a major hadn't been determined. Eventually computers became my major, with physics and math as minors. One of the problems was that in the entire University of Helsinki there was only one other Swedish-speaking student who wanted to major in computers, Lars Wirzenius. The two of us joined Spektrum, the social organization for Swedish-speaking science students, which actually turned out to be a lot of fun. The club was comprised of students in the hard sciences, such as physics and chemistry. Translation: It's all guys.

But we did share our clubroom with the counterpart organization for Swedish-speaking students in the soft sciences, such as biology and psychology. That way, we were able to interact with females, as awkward as it might have been for some of us. Okay, all of us.

Spektrum had many of the trappings of an American-style

fraternity, but you didn't have to live with the other guys or ever deal with anyone who wasn't interested in science. We had regular Wednesday night meetings where I learned the difference between a pilsner and an ale. On rare occasions there were vodka-ingesting contests. But much of that didn't happen until later in my university career. And there was ample time for it to happen: I studied at the university for eight years, emerging with nothing more than a mere master's degree. (I'm not counting the honorary doctorate the university issued to me in June 2000.)

But that first year was a blur of streetcar commutes between lecture classes and my bedroom, which was gathering piles of books and computer equipment. I'd lie in bed reading a Douglas Adams sci-fi thriller, then toss it on the floor and pick up a physics text, then roll out of bed and sit at the computer writing a program for a new game. The kitchen is right outside the bedroom and I'd stumble in for some coffee or corn crunchies.

Maybe your sister is somewhere around, or maybe she is out with friends. Or maybe she is living with your father these days. Maybe your mother is there or maybe she is working or maybe she is out with her journalist friends. Or a friend is over and you are wedged into the kitchen, drinking cup after cup of tea and watching Bevis and Butthead in English on MTV and thinking about going somewhere to play snooker but it is just too cold outside.

And happily, there is no phys ed in this lifetime.

That will happen next year. All year. When the Finnish Army calls every male. Many guys do their army duty immediately following high school. For me, instead, it seemed to make more sense to wait until after completing a year at the university.

In Finland you have a choice: You either do the army for eight months or social services for a year. If you show strong religious reasons or some other significant excuse, you could get around both. For me, there wasn't such an out. And the option of social services didn't feel right.

It wasn't because I had anything against helping humanity. It probably had more to do with a fear that social services duty ran the risk of actually being *more* boring than army duty. I can't believe I'm being so candid. But talk to someone who has gone the social services route and you find that if you haven't already lined up a good place to perform them, you will be randomly assigned to an uninteresting place. And I couldn't conscientiously object. As much as I wouldn't have objected to shirking my patriotic duty, the fact is I actually do have a conscience: When push comes to shove, I don't have strong convictions against guns or killing people.

So if you opt for the army there are two new choices to make. You could go for the required eight months as a regular Joe, or go to officer training school and do eleven months as an officer. It occurred to me that it might be slightly more interesting to be an officer, despite the additional 129,600 minutes. It would also be a way of getting something more out of it.

That's how your (then) 120-pound hero became a second lieutenant in the reserves of the Finnish Army. My job was fire controller. It's not exactly rocket science. You are given the coordinates for the big guns. You read the map of where you are and then you triangulate on where you want to shoot. You do the coordinates calculations and then you radio them in or communicate using telephone wire that you helped lay out. You're telling the guns where to shoot.

I remember being very nervous before going into the army, not knowing what to expect. Some people had older brothers or someone to talk to about the army, so they knew what to anticipate. There was nobody to tell me what would be happening. Well, everybody knows in general that the army isn't going to be fun. It's something perpetuated by everybody being there. But I didn't have a clear idea of what it would be like, and that made me nervous. It's sort of how I feel about having people read this book.

The most difficult times in the army involve walking around the Lapland woods with what seem like tons of cable. Frankly, I think it *is* tons of cable. Before officers school, you would be ordered to run around with a huge roll of cable on your stomach and two on your back, and you have to run for, like, ten freaking miles. Other times you're just standing around waiting for things to happen.

Or you ski for too long to the place where you put up the tent. That's when I realized that if God had meant us to ski, He/She/It would have equipped us with elongated fiberglass pads instead of feet. Wait a second, I don't necessarily believe in God.

Then you have to get the tent set up and the fire going before you can eat. You're cold and hungry and tired because you haven't slept in two days. I understand that people actually pay good money to participate in such extreme outdoor adventures as "character-building experiences." They should just join the Finnish Army.

Actually, the outdoor marathons didn't happen often, but they happened. I calculated that during eleven months with the army, I spent more than 100 days in the woods. Finland has abundant woods: 70 percent of the country is covered with forest. I felt as if I visited it all.

My job as an officer was to be the fire control leader for a group of five. That just means you're supposed to know how things work, and make them seem more complicated than they really are. But it just wasn't that interesting and I wasn't a very good leader. I certainly wasn't good at giving orders. I took them well—the trick is not to take it personally—but I didn't feel that it was my mission in life to do the best job.

Not then.

Did I mention how cold it gets in Lapland?

Come to think of it, I really hated it while I was there. But it was one of those things: After it was over it immediately became a wonderful experience.

It also gave me something to discuss with virtually any Finnish male for the rest of my life. In fact, some people suggest that the major reason for the required army duty is to give Finnish men something to talk about over beer for as long as they live. They all have something miserable in common. They hated the Army, but they're happy to talk about it afterward.

VII.

While we're on the subject, let me tell you some more about Finland. We probably have more reindeer than any place on Earth. We also have a healthy share of both alcoholics and fans of tango dancing. Spend a winter in Finland and you understand the roots of all the drinking. There's no excuse for the tangoistas, but, thankfully, they are all pretty much concentrated in small towns, where you never have to encounter them.

A recent survey determined that Finnish males are the most virile in Europe. It must be all the reindeer meat, or the hours spent in saunas. This is a nation that literally is home to more saunas than cars. Nobody actually knows how this religion started, but the tradition, at least in some places, is to build the sauna first, then the house. Many apartment buildings contain a sauna on the first-floor level or the top floor, and every family gets its own private hour—like Thursdays, 7 to 8 P.M. (Thursdays and Fridays tend to be sauna days.) That way, you don't have to endure the horror of seeing your neighbors naked. I was once thumbing through an English-language guidebook to Finland that went to great lengths to warn the reader that Finns never have sex in saunas, and how they would be horrified to learn that such a violation has taken place or was even a mere fantasy in the tourist's mind. I couldn't stop laughing when I read that, because the sauna is such a neutral place in the Finnish home that the book might just as appropriately have warned against having sex on the kitchen floor. I don't think it's any big deal. In remote locales babies are born in saunas—the only places with hot water—and that's where you go to die, according to some traditions. These rules don't apply to my family, by the way, which has a laid-back approach to the whole thing.

There are other traits that distinguish Finns from other members of the human species. For example, there's this silence tradition. Nobody talks much. They just sort of stand around not saying anything. This is another rule that doesn't apply to my family, which I will generously describe as "offbeat."

Finns are stoic to a fault. Silent suffering and fierce determination might be what helped us survive in the face of domination by Russia, a succession of bloody wars, and weather that sucks. But these days, it just seems odd. The German writer Bertolt Brecht lived briefly in Finland during World War II and made the famous observation about patrons of a railway station café there "remaining silent in two languages." He left for the United States via Vladivostock the first chance he could.

Even today, if you step into a bar in any Finnish city—particularly the smaller ones—you're likely to find stone-faced men sitting by themselves, staring off into the air. People respect each other's privacy in Finland—that's another big thing—so nobody would think of going up to a stranger and striking up a conversation. There's a conundrum. Finns actually are quite friendly. But few people are ever able to find that out.

I understand the atmosphere is much more convivial in Finland's lesbian bars.

Since Finns are loathe to converse face to face, we represent the ideal market for mobile phones. We have taken to the new devices with an enthusiasm unmatched by any other nation. It's not clear which country actually does claim the most reindeer per capita—the title might go to Norway, come to think of it—but there's no question which nation on Earth has more cell phones for every man, woman, and child. There's talk in Finland of having them grafted to the body upon birth.

And they are used for more purposes than anywhere else.

Finns routinely send each other text messages, or rely on mobile phones as a mechanism for cheating on high school tests (send a friend the question and wait for his text-message reply). We use the calculator function that few Americans even realize exists on a mobile phone. The obvious next step is for folks to start dialing up the number of the lonely person at the next café table and strike up a cell conversation. The phenomenal success of Nokia notwithstanding, mobile phones have changed Finland like nothing since the introduction—long forgotten—of the sauna itself.

It's actually no surprise that mobile phones would find such a warm reception in Finland. The country has a history of being quick and confident in the adoption of technology. For example, unlike practically everywhere else on Earth, Finland is a place where folks routinely pay bills and conduct all their banking electronically—none of this wimpy pseudo-electronic banking that takes place in the United States. There are more Internet nodes per capita in Finland than any other country. Some credit this techno-savvy to the strong educational system—Finland has the world's highest literacy rate, and university tuition is free, which is why the typical student sticks around for six or seven years. Or, in my case, eight years. You can't help learning something by hanging around a university for such a large chunk of your life. Others say the technological edge got its start with the infrastructure improvements made in the shipping industry as part of war reparations paid to Russia. And others say it has something to do with a population that is (at times, unbearably) homogeneous.

*Linus and I are sitting at the diningroom table. We have just returned
from a car-racing/batting-cage place. Tove is putting away groceries,
Patricia and Daniela are in a tussle over a book I brought for one of
them. I brush aside a stuffed penguin and a huge jar of peanut butter,
turn on the tape recorder, and ask Linus to talk about his childhood.*

*"Actually, I don't remember much of my childhood," he says, in
a monotone.*

"How can that be? It was only a few years ago!"

*"Ask Tove. I'm lousy at remembering names or faces or what I did.
I have to ask her what our phone numbers are. I remember rules and how
things are organized, but I can never remember details of things, and I
don't remember the details of my childhood. I don't remember how things
happened or what I was thinking when I was small."*

"Well, did you have friends, for example?"

*"A few. I never was very social. I'm way, way more social now
than I was back then."*

*"Well, what was it like? I mean, do you remember waking up
on a Sunday morning and going somewhere with your sister and your
parents?"*

"My parents were split up by then."

"How old were you when they split up?"

"I don't know. Maybe six. Maybe ten. I don't remember."

"What about Christmas? Do you remember Christmas?"

"Oh, I have some vague memories of getting dressed up and going to

34

my paternal grandfather's house in Turku. Same thing for Easter. Other than that I don't remember much."

"What about your first computer?"

"That was the famed VIC-20 my maternal grandfather bought. It came in a box."

"How big was the box? The size that would hold a pair of snow boots?"

"About that size."

"And what about your grandfather? Do you remember much about him?"

"He was probably my closest relative but I don't . . . Okay. He was overweight, but not fat. He was balding. He was withdrawn, sort of like an absent-minded professor, which he was. I used to sit on his lap and type in his programs."

"Can you remember what he smelled like?"

"No. What kind of a question is that?"

"Everybody's grandfather smells like something. Cheap cologne. Bourbon. Cigars. What did he smell like?"

"I don't know. I was too preoccupied with the computer to notice."

Birth of an
OPERATING
SYSTEM*

*Warning: Intermediate geek language until page 119.

I.

Some people remember time according to the cars they drove or the jobs they held or the places they lived or the sweethearts they dated. My years are marked by computers.

I had only three computers while I was growing up. There was the aforementioned Commodore VIC-20, which I inherited from my grandfather. It was one of the first "home" computers, the predecessors to the present-day PCs. The Commodore 64 became sort of the big brother to the VIC-20, followed by the Amiga, which had a particularly strong following in Europe. Those computers never became truly popular, like the PC or even the Apple II, which was already common about the time I played around with the VIC.

In those days before the proliferation of PCs, most of the programming on home computers was done in assembly language. (I can't believe I've taken to starting sentences with "In those days . . .") Computers had their own home-brew operating system, the equivalent of what DOS was on a PC. Depending on the computer, it was either a rudimentary format or a slightly more enhanced one. Like DOS, the OS had a program loader and a basic language environment. Back then there were no standards and a number of companies wanted to control the market. Commodore was one of the better known of these.

When I had gotten about as much as I could out of the VIC-20, I started saving up for a next-generation model. This was a big deal in my life. As I mentioned, I've lost track of who in my family was living where at what particular time, and a lot of other things, but the path to my second computer was something that's hard to forget.

I had some Christmas-and-birthday money stashed away (because I was born on December 28th, the two occasions are sort of melded together). I also earned some money one summer working on the clean-up crew in Helsinki's parks. Many of the parks in Helsinki aren't landscaped and well-maintained, but are more like recreational or green areas that are overgrown forests. What we had to do was saw off overgrown bushes or pick up dead branches—it was even interesting. I've always liked the outdoors. I also had a newspaper route, too, at one point—except that it wasn't newspapers, it was junk mail. Actually, I wasn't really into summer jobs, come to think of it. But I did them in those days. On the whole, I probably got more money from school stipends.

In Finland, it's relatively common for people to give endowments to schools, even the public elementary schools. So, starting in fourth grade, money gets distributed to students based on whatever the person setting up the fund had in mind. I remember one of the endowments in my school went to the best-liked kid in class. This was in sixth grade and we actually voted within the class on who should get the money. It wasn't me who won, I might add. The bounty amounted to only about 200 Finnmarks, which was maybe forty dollars, at the time, but it seemed like a lot of money to give a sixth grader just for being popular.

Quite often the money went to the best person in a particular subject or sport. And a lot of the awards were school-specific or funded through the government. In some cases, the funds dwindled over time. I remember one that amounted to about a penny in value. When that was the situation, the school would chip in to make it somewhat more useful, but it still was a fairly small sum of money; more than anything else, this was a way of maintaining the tradition of giving out money every year. Finland takes its academic traditions seriously, which is a good thing.

So I would receive these stipends every year for being the

Math Guy. By high school the awards got bigger. The biggest ones were on the order of $500. So that's where most of the money for my second computer came from; my weekly allowance wouldn't have paid for a computer. I also borrowed some money from my dad.

It was 1986 or 1987. I was sixteen or seventeen. My basket- ball years were behind me. I spent an inordinate amount of time researching the field before deciding which computer to buy. PCs weren't very good back then, so when I fantasized about my new machine I knew it wasn't going to be a PC.

I opted for a Sinclair QL, which many of you are probably too young to remember. Here's the history. The Sinclair was one of the first 32-bit machines on the market for home use. Sir Clive Sinclair, the founder of the company, was the Steve Wosniak of Britain. He made these computer kits that were sold as Timex computers in the United States. That's right, the same company that made Timex watches imported the Sinclair computer stuff and sold it here under the Timex name. The early ones were sold as kits before he started selling ready-made computers.

The Sinclair had this operating system called Q-DOS. I knew it by heart back then. It was written especially for that particular computer. It had quite an advanced Basic for the time, and fairly good graphics. One of the things that excited me the most about the operating system was that it was multitasking: You could run multiple programs at once. However, the Basic part wasn't multitasking, so you couldn't run more than one Basic program at once. But if you wrote your own programs in assembly language, you could let the operating system schedule them and time slice it so you could run many of them at the same time.

The computer contained the 8-megahertz 68008 chip, which was the second and cheaper version of Motorola's 68000 chip. Internally, the first generation of 68000 chips were 32-bit, but externally had a 16-bit interface to anything outside the CPU (central processing unit)—such as memory or hardware add-ons. Because it could only load 16 bits at a time from memory, 16-bit operations were often quicker than the 32-bit operations. The architecture was hugely popular and it still exists today in a lot of embedded devices or cars. It's not the same chip, but it's based on the same architecture.

The 68008 chip, the version in my computer, used 8 bits, not 16 bits, for its interface with the world outside the CPU. But even though it interacted with the outside world at 8 bits at a time, internally it was 32 bits. That made it more pleasant to program in many ways.

It had 128 kilobytes of memory—not megabytes—which was huge at the time for a home machine. The VIC-20 it replaced had only 3½ kilobytes of memory. And because it was a 32-bit machine it could access all the memory with no problem at all, which was unheard of back then. That was the main reason I wanted to buy the computer. The technology was interesting and I loved the CPU.

I was hoping to get the computer at a discount by buying it at a store where a friend knew the owners. But it would have taken so long for the computer to arrive that I just shlogged down to Akademiska Bokhandeln, the largest bookstore in Helsinki, which had a computer section. I just bought it from them over the counter.

The computer cost nearly $2,000. There used to be this rule that entry-level computers were always $2,000. It's only in the last couple of years that this has changed. Now you can buy a new PC for $500. It's like cars. Nobody makes cars for under $10,000. At some point, it's not worth it anymore. Sure, companies can build a car that can be sold for $7,000, but the automakers reason that people who could afford $7,000 for a car are happier buying one for $10,000 that has extra stuff, like air conditioning, as standard equipment. If you compare entry-level cars this year with entry-level cars from fifteen years ago, they cost about the same. In fact, adjusted for inflation they might cost slightly less. But they're a lot better.

That's how it used to be with computers. When computers were not something that everybody bought, there was a pain threshold of around $2,000. If the lowest-cost computer is much more expensive, a company isn't going to be able to sell many of them. But they were expensive enough to manufacture that it didn't make sense for a company to make them much cheaper. People would always pay the extra $200 or so to get a better machine.

In the last two years they have become a lot less expensive to make. And even the low-end machines have gotten pretty good. Companies have lost many of the people who would pay the extra $200 for a slightly better machine. Since companies couldn't sell on features alone, they've had to sell on price.

I admit it: Back in 1987, one of the selling points of the QL was that it *looked* cool.

It was entirely matte black, with a black keyboard. It was fairly angular. This was not a rounded, pretty-boy machine. It tried to be kind of extreme. The keyboard was about an inch thick because it was part of the same unit as the computer. That's the way most of the home computers were designed. On the right-hand side of the keyboard, where you would have a keypad, you had two slots for the revolutionary Sinclair microdrive, which was this endless loop of tape that was used only on a Sinclair machine. It acted and was organized like a disk drive. Because it was one long loop, you could just spin it until you hit what you wanted. It turned out to be a bad idea because it was not as reliable as a disk drive.

So I spent close to $2,000 for the Sinclair QL. Most of what I did with it was one programming project after another. I was always searching for something interesting to do. I had a Forth language interpreter and compiler, just to play around with. Forth was a strange language that nobody uses anymore. It was kind of a fun, niche-market language that was fairly widely used in the 1980s for different things, but it never became very popular, being difficult to follow for non-techie people. Actually it was kind of useless.

I wrote programming tools for myself. One of the first things I bought for the machine was an expansion bay with an

EEPROM card (Electrically Erasable and Programmable Read Only Memory). It's memory you write yourself with special modules, and it stays around when you turn the power off. That way, I could have the tools easily available to me whenever I wanted, without having to load them into RAM (random access memory) and use precious RAM for programs.

What got me interested in operating systems: I bought a floppy controller so I wouldn't have to use the microdrives, but the driver that came with the floppy controller was bad so I ended up writing my own. In the process of writing that I found some bugs in the operating system—or at least a discrepancy between what the documentation said the operating system would do and what it actually did. I found it because something I had written didn't work.

My code is always, um, perfect. So I knew it had to be something else, and I went in and disassembled the operating system.

You could buy books that contain partial listings of the operating system. That helps. You also need a disassembler, a tool that takes the machine language and turns it into assembly language. That's important because when you only have a machine language version, it's difficult to follow the instructions. You find that an instruction will jump to a numerical address, which makes it very hard to read. A good disassembler will make up names for the numbers and also allow you to specify names. It also can be used to help you identify particular instruction sequences. I had my own disassembler that I could use to create reasonably nice listings. When something didn't work, I could go in and tell it to find the listing from a particular spot, and I could see everything that the operating system was going to do. Sometimes I used the disassembler not because something was buggy but because I was trying to understand what it was supposed to do.

One of the things I hated about the QL was that it had a read-only operating system. You couldn't change things. It did have hooks—places where you can insert your own code to take over certain functions—but only at particular places. It's so much nicer to be able to replace your operating system completely. Doing an operating system in ROM (read-only memory) is a bad idea.

Despite what I've said about Finland being such a technology butt-kicker, the Sinclair QL wasn't making big inroads in Europe's seventh-largest nation. Because the market was so small, whenever you wanted to buy upgrades for the iconoclastic, leading-edge machine, you had to do it from England, via postal order. It involved scouring catalogues until you found someone who sold whatever it was you wanted. Then you had to get together certified checks and wait weeks for delivery (this being before the days of Amazon.com and credit cards). That's what I had to do when I wanted to expand my RAM from 128 kilobytes to 640 kilobytes. That was the drill when I bought a new assembler, to translate assembly language into machine code (the ones and zeros), and an editor, which is basically a word-processing program for programming.

Both the new assembler and editor worked fine, but they were on the microdrives and couldn't be put on the EEPROM. So I wrote my own editor and assembler and used *them* for all my programming. Both were written in assembly language, which is incredibly stupid by today's standards. It's complicated and time-consuming—I'd guess it takes a hundred times longer to solve a problem in assembly language than in the C language, for example, which was available at the time.

I added a few commands to the basic interpreter that came with the machine so that when I wanted to edit something I basically just ran my editor automatically and it was instantly there. My editor was faster than the one that came with the machine. I was particularly proud of how fast I could write characters to the screen. Normally, with a machine like that, it would take so long to fill the screen with characters that you could see text scroll. And I was pleased with the fact that with my editor, you wrote text so fast that when you scrolled quickly down you created a blur. That was important to me. The improvement made the machine feel much snappier, and I knew that I had done a lot of work to make it operate so fast.

At this time, there weren't very many people I knew who were as involved in computers as I was. There was a computer club at school, but I didn't spend much time there. It was basically for kids who wanted to know about computers. There were only about 250 students in my entire high school, and I don't think anybody else had been using one since the age of ten.

One of the big things I liked doing on my Sinclair QL was to make clones of games. I wrote clones of the games from the VIC-20 that I had enjoyed and sometimes I added enhancements. But mostly they were not better: a better machine, not a better concept.

My favorite game was probably Asteroids, but I could never make a good clone of it. The reason was that, at the time, all the arcade Asteroids games were done with real vector graphics. Instead of having graphics based on small dots—pixels—they had graphics that were actually done the way a cathode-ray tube (CRT) works, which is to have electrons shot out from an electron cannon from behind the CRT and deflected with magnets. They got much higher-resolution graphics that way, but you couldn't reproduce this very easily. You could make a clone, but it wouldn't look like the original Asteroids game if you wrote it on a computer that didn't have the special graphics capability.

I remember making a Pac Man clone in assembly language. The first step is to kind of remember what the Pac Man characters are supposed to look like. Then you try to draw them on a sixteen-by-sixteen grid of paper, with color. And if you are artistic, you can do a good job. But if you are Mr. Non-Artistic, like I am, it ended up looking like Pac Man's sick cousin.

Okay, so it wasn't a very good clone. But I was really proud of it. The game was actually playable, and I sent it in to one of the magazines that published computer code. I had sold other programs to magazines and thought this would be a natural.

Not.

One of the problems was that the program had been written in assembly language. That meant that if you made the slightest, *slightest* mistake copying it from the magazine, it wouldn't work.

I wrote some of my own games, too. But it takes a certain mindset to create games. Because games require a lot of performance, you have to get really low down into the hardware of the computer. I could do that, but I didn't have the game play mentality. What makes a great game is not usually how fast it is or how good the graphics are. There has to be something that makes you play it—something that keeps you with it. It's just like movies. Special effects are one thing, but you also need a plot. And my games never had a plot. A game has to have a progression, an idea. Often, the progression is just that the game gets faster. That's what Pac Man does. Sometimes the maze changes or the monsters get better at following you.

One of the things that interested me about Pac Man was tackling the problem of making graphics that don't flicker. It's a fairly common problem in older computer games, because without special hardware your characters just flicker. The way you move your characters around is to take away the old copy and write a new copy. If you happen to have bad timing, people can actually see when there's no copy, so it flickers. You can get around this in multiple ways. You can actually draw the new guy first and *then* remove the old guy, but you must be careful not to remove that part of the old guy that was occluded by the new guy. Instead of seeing an irritating flicker, you get a good effect—you sometimes see the shadow of the old character on the screen. The brain interprets that in a good way. It doesn't flicker, but it creates a motion blur. The trouble with this solution is that it is fairly expensive and time-consuming to create.

There's a reason that games are always on the cutting edge, and why they often are the first types of programs that programmers create. Partly it has to do with the fact that some of the smartest programmers out there are fifteen-year-old kids playing around in their rooms. (It's what I thought sixteen years ago, and I still suspect it's true.) But there's another reason games are so pioneering: Games tend to push hardware.

If you look at computers today, they're usually fast enough

for anything. But the place you test the limits of the hardware are with action games, like some of the 3-D ones that are now popular. Fundamentally, games are one of the few things on computers where you can tell if things aren't happening in real time. In word processing, you don't mind a delay of a second here or a second there. But in a game, it starts to be noticeable at a sub-tenth of a second. Games used to be fairly simple. These days, programming is actually a fairly small part of any game. There's music, there's the plot. If you compare it to making a movie, the programming component is just the camera work.

So I had the Sinclair QL for three years. It took me from high school to the University of Helsinki to the Finnish Army. It was fine, but we were definitely ready to part ways. In the last year or so I had discovered its shortcomings. The 68008 was a good enough CPU, but I was reading about the next generation 68020, and learning about such virtues as memory management and paging. These new computers could do things that are really important when you are working on low-level stuff.

What irritated me about the Sinclair QL was that while the operating system was capable of multitasking, you could still crash at any time because there was no memory protection. One task that decided to do something bad could just crash the machine.

The Sinclair QL was Sir Clive Sinclair's last foray into designing and making computers. One of the reasons: It wasn't commercially successful. It had interesting technology, but the company had production problems and quality assurance problems and the inevitable bad press. Moreover, the market was beginning to become more competitive.

The late 1980s were the years when you could start to imagine that, yes, maybe someday your average trolley rider would own a computer, if only to perform word processing. And all signs pointed to the PC. Yes, the original IBM PCs had started flooding the shelves and becoming successful despite numerous technical shortcomings. Those ubiquitous beige creatures had the IBM stamp of approval, after all, and that meant a lot. Another attraction: The peripherals were standard and easy to obtain.

I was reading about all these newer CPUs that *could* do what I wanted. It became clear that the 68020, which *looked* interesting, wasn't going anywhere. I could have considered buying a CPU upgrade for the QL. In those days that meant basically rebuilding the machine. And the operating system didn't know about memory management, anyway, so I would have had to write my own version. So it was like: *Hhhmmm. Doing that will be a big step. And it will be expensive to get a new CPU.*

And then there was still the increasing headache of buying things for the computer. It wasn't as if there was a Sears catalogue for the Sinclair QL and you just picked up the phone and ordered more memory. The postal-order-from-England routine was getting old. (I didn't mind that there was no shrink-wrapped software because I was able to write all that myself.)

There was a positive side effect to this pain-in-the-neck. When I was thinking about getting rid of the machine, I decided to sell my peripherals—the real hard drive I had purchased because I couldn't take the microdrive one second longer, and my expansion RAM. But there weren't people lined up in the streets searching for such stuff, so you had to advertise in a computer magazine and pray. And that's how I met my good friend Jouko Vierumaki, who turned out to be probably the only other person in all of Finland who owned a Sinclair QL. He answered my ad and took the train from Lahti and bought some of my peripherals. Then he introduced me to snooker.

II.

My first year at university, the Sinclair QL sat on a desk against my first-floor bedroom window on Petersgatan, but I didn't do much in the way of programming. Partly it was a matter of wanting to concentrate on my studies. But also, I simply found myself lacking a project to do on my computer. Lack a project and you lack enthusiasm. You're trying to come up with something that might motivate you.

It seemed like the perfect time to join the army, which I knew I would have to do anyway. I was nineteen years old and irritated with my computer's shortcomings and unattached to any interesting computer project. I boarded a train for Lapland.

I've already indicated how clueless I was about, among other things, the physical demands of army service. So after the eleven months of phys ed-with-firearms, I felt perfectly justified in spending the remaining decades of my life in blissful inactivity, with the only exercise coming from tapping code into a keyboard or gripping my fingers around a glass of pilsner. (In fact, the first near-sport activity after leaving the army didn't take place until almost ten years to the day following my discharge, when David coerced me into going boogie-boarding with him in the killer waves at Half Moon Bay. I practically drowned, and my legs were sore for days.)

Army service ended on the 7th of May, 1990. Although Tove would tell you I have trouble remembering our anniversary, I can't possibly forget the date I was discharged.

The first thing I wanted to do was get a cat.

I had a friend whose cat had produced a litter a few weeks earlier, so I bought the sole remaining kitten, which was white, male, beautiful—and, because he had spent his first few weeks in the outdoors, easily able to live both inside and outside my mother's apartment. I named him Randi, short for Mithrandir, the white wizard in *Lord of the Rings*. He is now eleven years old and, like his owner, has become totally adjusted to the California lifestyle.

No, I don't think I did anything productive that entire summer. Classes for my second year at the university wouldn't start until fall. My computer was not quite up to snuff. So I sort of hung around in my ratty bathrobe or played with Randi or, occasionally, got together with friends so they could chuckle about my attempts at bowling or snooker. Okay, I did do a little fantasizing about my next computer.

I faced a geek's dilemma. Like any good computer purist raised on a 68008 chip, I despised PCs. But when the 386 chip came out in 1986, PCs started to look, well, attractive. They were able to do everything the 68020 did, and by 1990, mass-market production and the introduction of inexpensive clones would make them a great deal cheaper. I was very money-conscious because I didn't have any. So it was, like, this is the machine I want to get. And because PCs were flourishing, upgrades and add-ons would be easy to obtain. Especially when it came to hardware, I wanted to have something that was standard.

I decided to jump over and cross the divide. And it would be fun getting a new CPU. That's when I started selling off pieces of my Sinclair QL.

Now everybody has a book that has changed his or her life. The Holy Bible. *Das Kapital. Tuesdays With Maury. Everything I Needed to Know I Learned in Kindergarten.* Whatever. (I sincerely hope that, having read the preface and my theory on The Meaning of Life, you will decide that this book does the trick for you.) The book that launched me to new heights was *Operating Systems: Design and Implementation,* by Andrew S. Tanenbaum.

I had already signed up for my fall courses, and the one that

I was most looking forward to was in the C programming language and the Unix operating system. In anticipation of the course, I bought the aforementioned textbook during the summer in the hope of getting a head start. In the book, Andrew Tanenbaum, a university professor in Amsterdam, discusses Minix, which is a teaching aid he wrote for Unix. Minix is also a small Unix clone. Soon after reading the introduction, and learning the philosophy behind Unix and what the powerful, clean, beautiful operating system would be capable of doing, I decided to get a machine to run Unix on. I would run Minix, which was the only version I could find that was fairly useful.

As I read and started to understand Unix, I got a big enthusiastic jolt. Frankly, it's never subsided. (I hope you can say the same about something.)

III.

The academic year that began in the fall of 1990 was to be the first time that the University of Helsinki would have Unix, the powerful operating system that had been bred in AT&T's Bell Labs in the late 1960s but had grown up elsewhere. In my first year of studies, we had a VAX running VMS. It was a horrible operating system, certainly not an environment that made you say, "Gee, I'd like to have this at home, too." Instead it made you say, "Hmmm. How do you do *that?*" It was hard to use. It didn't have many tools. It wasn't suited to easily accessing the Internet, which was running on Unix. You couldn't even easily figure out how large a file was. Admittedly, VMS was very well suited for certain operations, like databases. But it's not the kind of operating system that you get excited about.

The university had realized it was time to move away from all that. Much of the academic world was then growing enamored of Unix, so the university acquired a MicroVAX running Ultrix, which was Digital Equipment Corporation's version of Unix. It was a way of testing the waters of Unix.

I was eager to work with Unix by experimenting with what I was learning in Andrew Tanenbaum's book, excited about all the things I could explore if I had a 386 PC. There was no way I could get together the 18,000 FIM to buy one. I knew that once the fall semester began, I would be able to use my Sinclair QL to access the university's new Unix computer until I could afford to buy a PC on which I could run Unix on my own.

So there were two things I did that summer. Nothing. And

read the 719 pages of *Operating Systems: Design and Implementation.* The red soft-cover textbook sort of lived on my bed.

The University of Helsinki sprang for a sixteen-user license for the MicroVAX. That meant admittance to the "C and Unix" course was limited to thirty-two students—I guess the thinking was that sixteen people would be using it by day, sixteen by night. Like the rest of us, the teacher was new to Unix. He admitted this up front, so it wasn't really a problem. But he would read the text only one chapter ahead of the students, whereas the students were sometimes skipping ahead by three chapters. So it became something of a game in which people tried to trip up the teacher by asking questions that related to things we would be learning three chapters later, just to see if he had read that far.

We were all babes in the Unix woods, with a course that was being made up as we went along. But what was obvious from this course was that there was a unique philosophy behind Unix. You grasped this in the first hour of the course. The rest was explaining the details.

What is special about Unix is the set of fundamental ideals that it strives for. It is a clean and beautiful operating system. It avoids special cases. Unix has the notion of processes—a process is anything that does anything. Here's a simple example. In Unix the shell command, which is what you type to gain entry into the operating system, is not built into the operating system, as with DOS. It's just a task. Like any other task. It just happens that this task reads from your keyboard and writes back to your monitor. Everything that does something in Unix is a process. You also have files.

This simple design is what intrigued me, and most people, about Unix (well, at least us geeks). Pretty much everything you do in Unix is done with only six basic operations (called "system calls," because they are the calls you make to the operating system to do things for you). And you can build up pretty much everything from those six basic system calls.

There's the notion of "fork," which is one of the fundamental Unix operations. When a process does a fork, it creates a complete copy of itself. That way, you have two copies that are the same. The child copy most often ends up *executing* another process—replacing itself with a new program. And that's the second basic operation. Then you have four other basic system calls: open, close, read, and write—all designed to access files. Those six system calls make up the simple operations that comprise Unix.

Sure, there are tons of other system calls to fill in all the details. But once you understand the six basic ones, you understand Unix. Because one of the beauties of Unix is realizing that you don't need to have complex interfaces to build up something complex. You can build up any amount of complexity from the interactions of simple things. What you do is create channels of communication (called "pipes" in Unix-speak) between simple processes to create complex problem-solving.

An ugly system is one in which there are special interfaces for everything you want to do. Unix is the opposite. It gives you the building blocks that are sufficient for doing everything. That's what having a clean design is all about.

It's the same thing with languages. The English language has twenty-six letters and you can build up everything from those letters. Or you have the Chinese language, in which you have one letter for every single thing you can think of. In Chinese, you start off with complexity, and you can combine complexity in limited ways. That's more of the VMS approach, to have complex things that have interesting meanings but can't be used in any other way. It's also the Windows approach.

Unix, on the other hand, comes with a small-is-beautiful philosophy. It has a small set of simple basic building blocks that can be combined into something that allows for infinite complexity of expression.

This, by the way, is also how physics works. You try and find the fundamental rules that are supposed to be fairly simple. The complexity comes from the many incredible interactions you get from those simple rules, not from any inherent complexity of the rules themselves.

The simplicity of Unix did not just happen on its own. Unix, with its notion of simple building blocks, was painstakingly designed and written by Dennis Richie and Ken Thompson at AT&T's Bell Labs. And you should absolutely not dismiss simplicity for something easy. It takes *design* and good taste to be simple.

To go back to the example of human languages: Pictorial writing like Chinese characters and hieroglyphics tend to happen first, and be "simpler," whereas the building block approach requires far more abstract thinking. In the same way, you should not confuse the simplicity of Unix with a lack of sophistication—quite the reverse.

Which is not to say that the original reasons for Unix were all that sophisticated. Like so many other things in computers, it was all about games. It took somebody who wanted to play computer games on a PDP-11. Because that was what UNIX started out being developed for—Dennis and Ken's personal project for playing Space Wars. And because the operating system wasn't considered a serious project, AT&T didn't think of it as a commercial venture. In fact, AT&T was a regulated monopoly, and one of the things they couldn't do was to sell computers anyway. So the people who created Unix made it available quite freely along with source licenses, especially to universities. It wasn't a big deal.

This all led to Unix becoming a big project in academic circles. By the time of the 1984 breakup, when AT&T was finally allowed to get into the computer business, computer scientists at universities—particularly the University of California-Berkeley—had been working on and improving Unix for years under the direction of people like Bill Joy and Marshall Kirk McKusik. People hadn't always necessarily put a lot of effort into documenting what they did.

But by the early 1990s, Unix had become the number-one operating system for all supercomputers and servers. It was huge business. One of the problems was that there were, by now, a host of competing versions of the operating system. Some were derived from the more controlled confines of the AT&T code base (the so-called "System V" flavors), while others were derived from the University of California-Berkeley code-base BSD (Berkeley Software Distribution). Yet others were a mixture of the two.

One BSD derivation in particular is worth mentioning. It was the 386BSD project done by Bill Jolitz based on the BSD code-base, distributed over the Internet. It was later to fragment and become the freely available BSD flavors—NetBSD, FreeBSD, and OpenBSD—and it was getting a lot of attention in the Unix community.

That's why AT&T woke up and sued the University of California-Berkeley. The original code had been AT&T's but most of the subsequent work had been done at Berkeley. The University of California regents contended that they had the right to distribute, or sell for a nominal fee, their version of Unix. And they demonstrated that they had done so much work that they essentially rewrote what AT&T had made available. The suit ended up being settled after Novell, Inc., bought Unix from AT&T. Essentially, parts of the system had to be excised from what AT&T had made available.

Meanwhile, all the legal haggling had been instrumental in giving a new kid on the block some time to mature and spread itself. Basically, it gave Linux time to take over the market. But I'm getting ahead of myself.

Since I'm digressing anyway, I'd like to explain something. Unix has this reputation for being a magnet for the eccentric fringe of computing. It's a reputation not worth arguing against. It's true.

Frankly, there *are* a lot of fairly crazy people in Unix. Not postal-rage crazy. Not poison-the-neighbor's-dog crazy. Just *very* alternative-lifestyle people.

Remember, much of the initial Unix activity took place in the late 1960s and early 1970s, while I was sleeping in a laundry basket in my grandparents' apartment. These were flower power people—but *technical* flower power people. A lot of the Unix-must-be-free philosophy has more to do with the circumstances of the time rather than with the operating system. It was a time of rampant idealism. Revolution. Freedom from authority. Free love (which I missed out on, and probably wouldn't have known what to do with, anyway). And the relative openness of Unix, even if it was mainly due to the lack of commercial interests of the time, made it attractive to this kind of person.

The first time I was introduced to this side of Unix was probably in 1991 or so when Lars Wirzenius dragged me along to an event at the Polytechnic University of Helsinki (which, as everybody knows, is not actually in Helsinki but right across the border in Espoo). They just want to be associated with the glamorous Helsinki even if only by name). The speaker was Richard Stallman.

Richard Stallman is the God of Free Software. He started to work on an alternative to Unix in 1984, calling it the GNU system. GNU stands for "GNU is Not Unix," being one of many recursive acronyms where one of the letters stands for the acronym itself—a kind of computer science in-joke that nobody else ever gets. Geeks—we're just tons of fun to be around.

More importantly, RMS, as he prefers to be called, also wrote the Free Software Manifesto, and the Free Software copyright license—the GPL (General Public License). Basically, he pioneered the notion of free source-code availability as something intentional, not just an accident, the way it happened with original Unix open development.

I have to admit that I wasn't much aware of the sociopolitical issues that were—and are—so dear to RMS. I was not really all that aware of the Free Software Foundation, which he founded, and all that it stood for. Judging from the fact that I don't remember much about the talk back in 1991, it probably didn't make a huge impact on my life at that point. I was interested in the technology, not the politics—I had had enough politics at home. But Lars was an ideologist, and I tagged along and listened.

In Richard I saw, for the first time in my life, the stereotypical longhaired, bearded hacker type. We don't much have them in Helsinki.

I may not have seen the light, but I guess something from his speech must have sunk in. After all, I later ended up using the GPL for Linux. There I go, getting ahead of myself again.

IV.

January 2, 1991. It was the first day the stores were open after Christmas and my twenty-first birthday, the two biggest cash-generating days on my calendar.

With my Christmas-and-birthday money in hand, I made this huge economic decision to buy a computer that would cost 18,000 FIM, which was about $3,500. I didn't have that kind of money, so the idea was to put down one third of the cost and buy the computer on credit. Actually, the computer cost 15,000 FM. The rest came from the financing charges that would be paid over three years.

It was at one of these small corner shops, sort of a mom-and-pop computer store, only in this case it was just pop. I didn't care about the manufacturer, so I settled on a no-name, white-box computer. The guy showed you a price list and a smorgasbord of what CPU was available, how much memory, what disk size. I wanted power. I wanted to have 4 megabytes of RAM instead of 2 megabytes. I wanted 33 megahertz. Sure, I could have settled for 16 megahertz, but no, I wanted top of the line.

You told them what you wanted and they would put it together for you. It sounds quaint in this era of the Internet and UPS shipments. You came back three days later to pick it up, but those three days felt like a week. On January 5th I got my dad to help me drive the thing home.

Not only was it no-name, it was also nondescript. It was a basic gray block. I didn't buy *this* computer because it looked cool.

It was a very boring-looking machine with a fourteen-inch screen, the cheapest, most reasonably studly box I could find. Incidentally, by "studly" I mean a powerful computer that a few people owned. I don't intend to make it sound so unappealing-yet-functional, sort of like a Volvo station wagon. But the fact is: I wanted something dependable and with easy access to the upgrades I would inevitably require.

The computer came with a cut-down version of DOS. I wanted to run Minix, the Unix variant, so I ordered it and the operating system took more than a month to make its way to Finland. Oh, you could buy the book on Minix from a computer store, but, since there was so little demand for the operating system itself, you had to order it from the bookstore. The cost was $169 plus taxes, plus conversion factor, plus whatever. I thought it was outrageous at the time. Frankly, I still do. The wasted month felt like about six years. I was even more frustrated by that than I had been during the months I was waiting to buy my PC.

And this was dead-winter. Every time you left your bedroom for the outside world you risked getting knocked onto the snow by old ladies who should have been home making cabbage soup for their families or watching hockey on television while knitting sweaters, not staggering along Mannerheimintie. I basically spent that month playing Prince of Persia on my new computer. When I wasn't doing that, I would read books that helped me understand the computer I had bought.

Minix finally arrived on a Friday afternoon, and I installed it that night. It required feeding sixteen floppy disks into the computer. The entire weekend was devoted to getting accustomed to the new system. I learned what I liked about the operating system—and, more importantly, what I didn't like. I tried to compensate for its shortcomings by downloading programs that I had gotten used to from the university computer. In all, it took me a month or more to make this my own system.

Andrew Tanenbaum, the professor in Amsterdam who wrote Minix, wanted to keep the operating system as a teaching aid. So it had been crippled on purpose, in bad ways. There were patches to Minix—improvements, that is—including a well-known patch made by a hacker in Australia named Bruce Evans, who was the God of Minix 386. His improvement made Minix much more usable on a 386. Before even getting the computer I had been following the Minix newsgroups online, so I knew from the very beginning that I wanted to run his enhanced version. But because of the licensing situation, you had to buy the real version of Minix and then do a lot of work to bootstrap Evans's patches. It was a fairly major thing to do.

There were a number of features that disappointed me with Minix. The biggest letdown was terminal emulation, which was important because it was the program I used to connect to the university computer. I relied upon terminal emulation whenever I wanted to dial up the university's computer to either work on the powerful Unix computer or just go online.

So I began a project to create my own terminal emulation program. I didn't want to do the project under Minix, but instead to do it at the bare hardware level. This terminal emulation project would also be a great opportunity to learn how the 386 hardware worked. As I mentioned, it was winter in Helsinki. I had a studly computer. The most important part of the project was to just figure out what this machine did and have fun with it.

Because I programmed to the bare metal I had to start off from the BIOS, which is the early ROM code that the computer boots into. The BIOS reads either the floppy or the hard disk, and in this case, I had my program on a floppy. The BIOS reads the first sector of the floppy and starts executing it. This was my first PC and I had to learn how all this was done. This all happens in what's called "real mode." But in order to take advantage of the whole CPU and get into 32-bit mode, you have to go into "protected mode." There's a lot of complicated setup you have to do to make this happen.

So to create a terminal emulation program this way, you need to know how the CPU works. In fact, part of the reason I wrote in assembly language was just to learn about the CPU. The other things you need to know are how to write to the screen, how to read keyboard input, how to read and write to the modem. (I hope I'm not losing any of the non-geeks who have steadfastly refused to leap ahead to page 120.)

I wanted to have two independent threads. One thread would read from the modem and then display on the screen. The other thread would read from the keyboard and write out to the modem. And there would be two pipes going both ways. This is called task-switching, and a 386 had hardware to support this process. I thought it was a cool idea.

My earliest test program was written to use one thread to write the letter A to the screen. The other thread wrote the letter B. (I know, it sounds unimpressive.) And I programmed this to happen a number of times a second. With the timer interrupt, I wrote it so that the screen would fill with AAAAAAAAA. Then, all of a sudden, it would switch to BBBBBBBBB. It's a completely useless exercise from any practical standpoint, but it was a good way of showing that my task-switching worked. It took maybe a month to do this because I had to learn everything as I was going along.

So ultimately I was able to change the two threads, the AAAAAAAA and BBBBBBB, so that one read from the modem and wrote to the screen, and the other read from the keyboard and wrote to the modem. I had my own terminal emulation program.

When I wanted to read news, I would put in my floppy and reboot the machine, and I would read news from the university computer using my program. If I wanted to make changes to improve the terminal emulation package, I would boot into Minix and use it for programming.

And I was very proud of it.

My sister Sara knew about my great personal accomplishment. I showed it to her and she looked at the screens of AAAAAA's and BBBBBBBB's for about five seconds; then she said "Good" and went away, unimpressed. I realized it didn't look like much. It's completely impossible to explain to somebody else that, while something may not look like much, a lot is going on in the background. It's about as impressive as showing somebody a stretch of road you've just filled in with tar. Probably the only other person who saw it was Lars, the other Swedish-speaking computer science major who started the same year I did.

It was March, maybe April, and if the snow was turning to slush on Petersgatan. I didn't know—or much care. I was spending most of my time in a bathrobe, huddled over my unattractive new computer, with thick black window shades shielding me from the sunlight, not to mention the outside world. I was eeking out the monthly payments for my PC, which was scheduled to be paid off in three years. What I didn't know was that I would only be sending in payments for another year. By then, I would have written Linux, which would be seen by many more people than just Sara and Lars. By that time, Peter Anvin, who works with me now at Transmeta, would have started a collection on the Internet to get my computer paid off.

Everybody knew I wasn't making any money on Linux. People just started saying, Let's start a collection to pay off Linus's computer.

It was wonderful.

I had absolutely no money. I always felt it was important to not have asked for money or begged for money, but the fact that it was simply given to me was . . . I'm getting choked up.

That's how Linux got started. With my test programs turning into a terminal emulation package.

Red Herring *magazine sends me to Finland to report on Oulu, the emerging high-tech center that is home to 141 startups despite its forbidding location a few hours' drive from the Arctic Circle. It's a good opportunity to hook up with Linus's parents and his sister, Sara, in Helsinki.*

His father, Nils (who goes by the name Nicke), meets me in the lobby of the Sokos Hotel Vaakuna, across the plaza from the Helsinki railway station. He is trim, wears thick glasses, bears Lenin's beard. He has recently ended his four-year assignment in Moscow for the Finnish Broadcasting Company and is now writing a book about Russia and deciding whether or not to take a post in Washington, a place he doesn't find interesting. Months earlier he had won a prestigious national journalism award, a commendation that his ex-wife Anna later would say "mellowed him considerably."

In the early evening he drives me in his Volvo V40 on a tour of Linus's snow-crusted neighborhoods, pointing out the solid building in which both father and son attended elementary school, driving past the grandparents' apartment where Linus lived in his first three months, and then the park-view building in which the family lived for the following seven years. Nicke had spent one of those years in Moscow studying to be a communist, when Linus was five years old. Next he points out the pale yellow apartment building in which Linus and his sister moved following the divorce—a street-level adult video store has replaced the electronics supply store of Linus's youth—and finally we drive past the most substantial of the structures, the five-story apartment block in which his maternal grandparents resided, the birthplace of Linux. Linus's mother,

Anna, still lives there. This could be Manhattan's Upper East Side in late December.

Nicke is funny, smart, self-deprecating, and shares a host of gestures with his son, like the way he cradles his chin in his hand when he talks. They also share a grin. Unlike his son he is a lifelong athlete— a socialist jock—who plays on a basketball team, runs five miles a day, and has taken to swimming distances in an icy lake early each morning. At fifty-five, he walks with the athletic confidence of someone maybe two thirds his age. Another trait he does not share with Linus: Nicke seems to have had a complicated romantic life.

We have dinner in a bustling restaurant in central Helsinki where Nicke talks about the difficulty Linus had growing up as the son of an overactive communist who was a frequent public speaker and at one point held a minor public office. He explains that Linus was often teased about his father's radical politics, and that some parents even refused to let him play with their children. For that reason, explains Nicke, his son made a constant effort to distance himself from the left-wing rhetoric that was the backdrop of his childhood. "He wouldn't let me discuss it. He would leave the room," Nicke says. "Or else he always made a point of having an opposing view. I know Linus was teased in school for having the wrong father. The message to me was, 'Don't put me in this awkward situation.'"

Nicke drives me to his home, where he says we will drink beer in his kitchen. It is north of the central business district, in a collection of buildings that were originally built in the 1920s to house workers. We ascend the steps to his apartment and remove our shoes in the entry. The place recalls the late 1960s counterculture, with woven-basket lampshades, third-world wall hangings, houseplants. We sit at the kitchen table, where Nicke pours beer and we talk about fathering. "A parent shouldn't think that it is he who makes his children what they are," he says, reaching for his mobile phone to dial up the woman with whom he lives. He indicates that Linus is just starting to read the historical books he has been bugging him to read for years, and that Linus probably has never bothered to read his own grandfather's poetry.

I ask Nicke if he has ever expressed an interest in programming,

ever asked Linus to show him the fundamentals. He tells me he never has.
Fathers and sons are unique individuals, he reasons, explaining that the
act of delving into Linus's passion would be akin to "invading his soul."
He seems comfortable in the role of father to a famous person. In a recent
newspaper profile following his winning of the national journalism
award, he was quoted as saying that, even in the days when he picked
Linus up from the playground, other kids would point and say, "Look,
there's Linus's father!"

    Sara Torvalds has traveled by train from her home in a small city
west of Helsinki, where the street signs are in Swedish first and Finnish
second, and where she can afford an apartment with a claw-foot tub and
sauna, and where, to her delight, Swedish—not Finnish—is heard on
the streets. As she explains, she is in a minority within a minority: as a
young adult she converted to Catholicism, an act that relegated her to the
10 percent of Finnish citizens who are non-Lutherans and caused her
agnostic father to disown her for a matter of weeks.
    Today she has traveled to Helsinki to teach catechism to youngsters
under a government-sponsored program. She is pleasant and upbeat, and
at twenty-nine she exudes the uncynical spirit of an earnest and busy high
schooler. Her fair skin and round face give her a vague resemblance to her
older brother, but it is obvious that she is naturally more sociable than he
is. She regularly taps the keys of her mobile phone to send text messages to
friends she will be meeting later in the day; then, just as frequently, she
checks for replies. She has a successful translation business.
    It is noon and Sara is taking me to meet her mother for lunch,
with stops at various childhood locales: the cat park, the elementary school.
"My parents were card-carrying communists, so that's how we were
brought up—to think the Soviet Union was a good thing. We visited
Moscow," she explains. "What I remember most was the huge toy store they
had, bigger than anything in Helsinki." Her parents divorced when she
was six. "I remember when we were told that Dad would be moving out
for good. I thought, That's good. Now the fighting will stop. Actually, he
had been going to Moscow for long periods, so we were used to him going

away," she says. By the time she was ten, Sara opted to move in with her father, who had relocated to the neighboring city of Espoo, rather than live with her mother and Linus. "It wasn't that I didn't want to live with Mom. It was just that I didn't want to live with Linus. That way we would only fight on weekends. We fought all the time. Little by little, we fought less as we grew older."

We arrive at her mother's first-floor apartment and Anna Torvalds is thrilled to see us. Mikke is her nickname. She refuses to let me indulge in the Finnish custom of removing one's shoes: "Don't be silly. This place is already dusty. You couldn't possibly make it worse." She is short, dark-haired, and extremely quick-witted. Within seconds of our arrival, the telephone rings. A real estate agent wants to show me the vacant apartment adjacent to Mikke's, so that I could describe it to her son in the United States and hand-deliver literature about it, in the event that he might want to purchase the place as a sort of Helsinki pied-a-terre. We enter the sprawling apartment, where the agent, who bears an eerie resemblance to the Annette Bening character in the film American Beauty, instructs us to slip little blue cloth booties over our shoes before we take the tour. Soon the agent, in an annoyingly cheerful tone, says something like, "Now this room here. It's a perfect room for antiques that you wouldn't want to have damaged by the sun." Mikke shoots me a conspiratorial glance and replies, in a mocking voice: "Oh, what a delightful way of telling us this room doesn't get any light."

Back in her own kitchen, Mikke sits at a rectangular table bearing a colorful tablecloth and pours coffee into an oversized mug. Her apartment, like that of her ex-husband, brims with books and folk art. There are black and white Marimekko curtains. The apartment originally contained three bedrooms and a kitchen. When her children moved out, Mikke moved into the large bedroom that had been occupied by Sara. She then dismantled the walls around Linus's room, and those around her original bedroom, to create a huge livingroom/kitchen. She points to a vacant spot and says, "That's where his computer was. I guess I should put up some sort of plaque. What do you think?" She chains smokes. She is an easy conversationalist, with such a solid command of English that there are no pauses when she delivers a phrase like, "He's not *some random shmuck you meet on the street." On the wall in her bedroom is a huge Soviet flag. It was a gift to Linus from Jouko Vierumaki, who had bought it during an international ski-jump competition. Linus had kept it in a drawer for years, but Mikke hung it above her bed.*

Mikke pulls out an album containing the family's few photographs. There's Linus at the age of two or three, naked on the beach. There's Linus, at the same age, shooting a moon outside a famous castle near Helsinki. There's Linus as an early adolescent, looking thin and awkward. There's Mikke at a sixtieth birthday party for her statistics-professor father. She points out her older sister and brother. "She's a New York psychiatrist. He's a nuclear physicist. And me, I'm the black sheep. Right? But I had the first grandchild," she declares, then lights a Gauloises.

We eat lunch at a restaurant named for Wilt Chamberlain. Sara consults her mobile phone while Mikke orders multiple espressos. Mikke recalls the way she and Nicke argued over whether Linus should or should not be forced to give up his pacifier: they wrote notes to each other and left them on the counter. There is talk about Linus's poor memory and his inability to remember faces. "If you're watching a movie with him and the hero changes his shirt from red to yellow, Linus will ask, 'Who is this guy?' " says Sara. There is talk about a family biking/camping vacation to Sweden. Sleeping on the overnight ferry. Having Sara's bicycle stolen the first day. Spending the budget on a new bicycle. Erecting the tent on a cliff. Leaving Linus inside to read all day while mother and daughter swam and fished. And then, after a powerful windstorm blew in, realizing that the only thing preventing the tent from being whisked into the Baltic Sea was Linus, who had been sleeping inside, oblivious to the extreme change in weather.

Mikke laughs as she relives the years in which Linus hid in his room, slaving away on a computer. "Nicke kept saying to me, 'Kick him out, make him get a job,' but Linus wasn't bothering me. He didn't require much. And whatever it was he was doing with his computer, that was his business, his thing, and he had a right to do it. I had no idea what it was all about."

Now she is as current as anyone on her son's activities. Mikke and the other family members are on the receiving end of a continual barrage of media queries. Those requests are forwarded to Linus, who typically responds by telling his mother, father, or sister to use their own judgment when answering. But after they write a response, they generally forward it to Linus for his approval before sending it on to the reporter.

Months earlier, when I emailed Mikke requesting her recollections of Linus's childhood, her response was lengthy and well-crafted. She titled her essay, "On Raising Linus from a Very Small Nerd." In it, she recounted her early observations that her toddler son showed the same signs of scientific determination she saw in her father and older brother:

"When you see a person whose eyes glaze over when a problem presents itself or continues to bug him or her, who then does not hear you talking, who fails to answer any simple question, who becomes totally engrossed in the activity at hand, who is ready to forego food and sleep in the process of working out a solution, and who does not give up. Ever. He—or she, of course—may be interrupted, and in the course of daily life often is, but blithely carries on later, single-mindedly. Then you know."

She wrote about the sibling rivalry between Linus and Sara, and about the irreconcilable differences. (Sara: "I don't LIKE the taste of mushrooms/liver/whatever." Linus: "YES YOU DO!") And the grudging respect. "Linus once expressed his awe of his sister very succinctly at an early age. He might have been five or seven or whatever, when he very seriously told me: 'You see. I don't think any new thoughts. I think thoughts that other people have thought, and I rearrange them. But Sara, she thinks thoughts that never were before.' "

These reminiscences may reveal that I still don't think Linus has any 'special' talent and certainly not 'for computers'—if it weren't that, it would be something else. In another day and age he would focus on some different challenge, and I think he will. (What I mean is, I hope he won't be stuck in Linux maintenance forever). For he is, I think, motivated not by 'computers,' and certainly not by fame or riches, but by honest curiosity and a wish to conquer difficulties as they arise, and to do it *the right way* because that's the way it IS and he won't give up.

I suppose I have already answered the question of what Linus was like as a son—easy to raise, yes. All he needed was a challenge and he did the rest. When he did start concentrating on computers as a youngster, it was even easier. As Sara and I used to say, just give Linus a spare closet with a good computer in it and feed him some dry pasta and he will be perfectly happy.

Except . . . and this is where my heart was in my throat when he was growing up: How on Earth was he going to meet any nice girls that way? I could only once more resort to the tried and true parenting measure of keeping my fingers crossed. And lo and behold: It worked! He met Tove while teaching at the university, and when she made him forget both his cat and his computer for several days, it was immediately obvious that Nature had triumphed, as is her wont.

I only hope the Ghouls of Fame won't distract him too much. (Fame seems not to have changed him, but he has mellowed, and now tends to talk to people when they approach him. He even seems to have difficulty saying no. But I suspect it has more to do with his having become a husband and father than with all the media hullabaloo).

And it's obvious that both mother and daughter stay abreast of that hullabaloo. It is late January 2000, the day following Transmeta's big public announcement of what it has been up to, and early in our lunch, Mikke asks Sara, "Was there anything in the paper today about you-know-who and you-know-what?"

That night, on her way to work, Mikke asks her taxi to wait outside my hotel while she drops off a pine child's chair she'd like me to hand-deliver to Patricia. That, and a floor plan of the available apartment for Linus.

About my first memory of Linus doing something remarkable.

I think it was early 1992. I was visiting Linus at his completely messy home once again—by bike and with no agenda. While watching MTV, as usual, I asked about Linus's operating-system development. Normally he answered something meaningless. This time, he led me to his computer (from Torvalds' messy kitchen to his totally chaotic room).

Linus gave the computer his username and password and got to a command prompt. He showed some basic functionality of the command interpreter—nothing special, though. After awhile, he turned to me with a Linus grin on his face and asked: "It looks like DOS, doesn't it?"

I was impressed and nodded. I wasn't stunned, because it looked like DOS too much—with nothing new, really. I should have known Linus never grins that way without a good reason. Linus turned back to his computer and pressed some function key combination—another login screen appeared. A new login and a new command prompt. Linus showed me four individual command prompts and explained that later they could be accessed by four separate users.

That was the moment I knew Linus had created something wonderful. I have no problem with that—I still dominate the snooker table.

Jouko "Avuton" Vierumaki

For me, it meant mainly that the phone lines were constantly busy and nobody could call us ... At some point, postcards began arriving from different corners of the globe. I suppose that's when I realized people in the real world were actually using what he had created.

Sara Torvalds

V.

The Beauty of Programming

I don't know how to really explain my fascination with programming, but I'll try. To somebody who does it, it's the most interesting thing in the world. It's a game much more involved than chess, a game where you can make up your own rules and where the end result is whatever you can make of it.

And yet, to the outside, it looks like the most boring thing on Earth.

Part of the initial excitement in programming is easy to explain: just the fact that when you tell the computer to do something, it will do it. Unerringly. Forever. Without a complaint.

And that's interesting in itself.

But blind obedience on its own, while initially fascinating, obviously does not make for a very likable companion. In fact, that part gets pretty boring fairly quickly. What makes programming so engaging is that, while you can make the computer do what you want, you have to figure out *how*.

I'm personally convinced that computer science has a lot in common with physics. Both are about how the world works at a rather fundamental level. The difference, of course, is that while in physics you're supposed to figure out how the world is made up, in computer science you *create* the world. Within the confines of the computer, you're the creator. You get to ultimately control everything that happens. If you're good enough, you can be God. On a small scale.

And I've probably offended roughly half the population on Earth by saying so.

But it's true. You get to create your own world, and the only thing that limits what you can do are the capabilities of the machine—and, more and more often these days, your own abilities.

Think of a treehouse. You can build a treehouse that is functional and has a trapdoor and is stable. But everybody knows the difference between a treehouse that is simply solidly built and one that is beautiful, that takes creative advantage of the tree. It's a matter of combining art and engineering. This is one of the reasons programming can be so captivating and rewarding. The functionality often is second to being interesting, being pretty, or being shocking.

It is an exercise in creativity.

The thing that drew me into programming in the first place was the process of just figuring out how the computer worked. One of the biggest joys was learning that computers are like mathematics: You get to make up your own world with its own rules. In physics, you're constrained by existing rules. But in math, as in programming, anything goes as long as it's self-consistent. Mathematics doesn't have to be constrained by any external logic, but it must be logical in and of itself. As any mathematician knows, you literally can have a set of mathematical equations in which three plus three equals two. You can do anything you want to do, in fact, but as you add complexity, you have to be careful not to create something that is inconsistent within the world you've created. For that world to be beautiful, it can't contain any flaws. That's how programming works.

One of the reasons people have become so enamored with computers is that they enable you to experience the new worlds you can create, and to learn what's possible. In mathematics you can engage in mental gymnastics about what might be. For example, when most people think of geometry, they think of Euclidean geometry. But the computer has helped people visualize different geometries, ones that are not at all Euclidean. With computers, you can take these made-up worlds and actually see what they look like. Remember the Mandelbrot set—the fractal images based on Benoit Mandelbrot's equations? These were visual representations of a purely mathematical world that could never have been visualized before computers. Mandelbrot just made up these arbitrary rules about this world that doesn't exist, and that has no relevance to reality, but it turned out they created fascinating patterns. With computers and programming you can build new worlds and sometimes the patterns are truly beautiful.

Most of the time you're not doing that. You're simply writing a program to do a certain task. In that case, you're not creating a new world but you are solving a problem within the world of the computer. The problem gets solved by thinking about it. And only a certain kind of person is able to sit and stare at a screen and just think things through. Only a dweeby, geeky person like me.

The operating system is the basis for everything else that will happen in the machine. And creating one is the ultimate challenge. When you create an operating system, you're creating the world in which all the programs running the computer live—basically, you're making up the rules of what's acceptable and can be done and what can't be done. Every program does that, but the operating system is the most basic. It's like creating the constitution of the land that you're creating, and all the other programs running on the computer are just common laws.

Sometimes the laws don't make sense. But sense is what you strive for. You want to be able to look at the solution and realize that you came to the right answer in the right way.

Remember the person in school who always got the right answer? That person did it much more quickly than everybody else, and did it because he or she didn't try to. That person didn't learn how the problem was *supposed* to be done but, instead, just thought about the problem the right way. And once you heard the answer, it made perfect sense.

The same is true in computers. You can do something the brute force way, the stupid, grind-the-problem-down-until-it's-not-a-problem-anymore way, or you can find the right approach and suddenly the problem just goes away. You look at the problem another way, and you have this epiphany: It was only a problem because you were looking at it the wrong way.

Probably the greatest example of this is not from computing but from mathematics. The story goes that the great German mathematician Carl Friedrich Gauss was in school and his teacher was bored, so to keep the students preoccupied he instructed them to add up all the numbers between 1 and 100. The teacher expected the young people to take all day doing that. But the budding mathematician came back five minutes later with the correct answer: 5,050. The solution is not to actually add up all the numbers, because that would be frustrating and stupid. What he discovered was that by adding 1 and 100 you get 101. Then by adding 2 and 99 you get 101. Then 3 and 98 is 101. So 50 and 51 is 101. In a matter of seconds he noticed that it's 50 pairs of 101, so the answer is 5,050.

Maybe the story is apocryphal, but the point is clear: A great mathematician doesn't solve a problem the long and boring way because he sees what the real pattern is behind the question, and applies that pattern to find the answer in a much better way. The same is definitely true in computer science, too. Sure, you can just write a program that calculates the sum. On today's computers that would be a snap. But a great programmer would know what the answer is simply by being clever. He would know to write a beautiful program that attacks the problem in a new way that, in the end, is the right way.

It's still hard to explain what can be so fascinating about beating your head against the wall for three days, not knowing how to solve something the better way, the beautiful way. But once you find that way, it's the greatest feeling in the world.

VI.

My terminal emulator grew legs. I was using it regularly to log onto the university computer and read email or participate in the discussions of the Minix newsgroup. The trouble is, I wanted to download things and upload things. That meant I needed to be able to save things to disk. In order to do that, my terminal emulator would require a disk driver. It also needed to get a file system driver, so that it would be able to look at the organization of the disk and save the stuff I was downloading as files.

That was the point where I almost gave up, thinking it would be too much work and not worth it. But there wasn't much else to do. I was going to classes that spring, and they weren't especially challenging. My sole outside activity was the weekly meeting (party) of Spektrum each Wednesday night. Social non-animal that I was, that became my only occasion to do anything other than program or study. Without those meetings (parties), I would have been a total recluse that spring, instead of a near-total recluse. Spektrum provided a built-in framework for a social life of some sort, and I don't think I ever missed one of their events. They were important to me—so important, in fact, that I sometimes lost sleep anticipating those meetings, hoping not to feel self-conscious about my lack of social graces or my nose or my obvious absence of a girlfriend. This is standard geek stuff.

What I'm trying to say is that I didn't have a heck of a lot of other interesting things going on. And the disk driver/file system driver project would be interesting. So I said, I'll do this. I wrote a disk driver. And because I wanted to save files to my Minix file system—and because the Minix file system was well-documented anyway—I made my file system compatible with the Minix file system. That way, I could read files I created under Minix and write them to the same disk so that Minix would be able to read the files I created from my terminal emulation thing.

This took a lot of work—a program-sleep-program-sleep-program-eat (pretzels)-program-sleep-program-shower (briefly)-program schedule. By the time I did this it was clear the project was on its way to becoming an operating system. So I shifted my thinking of it as a terminal emulator to thinking of it as an operating system. I think the transition occurred in the hypnosis of one of those marathon programming sessions. Day or night? I can't recall. One moment I'm in my threadbare robe hacking away on a terminal emulator with extra functions. The next moment I realize it's accumulating so many functions that it has metamorphosed into a new operating system in the works.

I called it my "gnu-emacs of terminal emulation programs." Gnu-emacs started out as an editor, but the people who created it built in a host of functions. They intended it to be an editor that can be programmed, but then the programmability part took over and it became the editor from hell. It contains everything but the kitchen sink, which is why sometimes the icon for the editor is actually a kitchen sink. It's known for being a huge piece of programming effort that has more functions than any editor needs. The same thing was happening with my terminal emulator. It was growing to be much more.

```
From: torvalds@klaava.Helsinki.Fi (Linus Benedict
   Torvalds)
To: Newsgroup: comp.os.minix
Subject: Gcc-1.40 and a posix question
Message-ID: <1991Jul3,100050.9886@klaava.Helsinki.Fi>
Date: 3 Jul 91 10:00:50 GMT
Hello Netlanders,
```

Due to a project I'm working on (in minix), I'm interested in the posix standard definition. Could somebody
please point me to a (preferably) machine-readable format of the latest posix rules? Ftp-sites would be nice.

Okay, this is the earliest public evidence that a geek in Finland was willing to test the bounds of his computing skill. The
POSIX standards are the lengthy rules for each of the hundreds of
system calls in Unix—what you need in order to get the computer
to perform its operations, starting with Read, Write, Open, Close.
POSIX is a Unix-standards body, an organization comprised of rep-
resentatives from companies that want to agree on common guide-
lines. Standards are important in order for programmers to be able
to write applications to the operating system and have them run on
more than one version. The system calls—particularly the important ones—would give me a list of the various functions needed for
an operating system. I would then write the code to make each of
those functions happen in my own way. By writing to the POSIX
standards, my code would be usable by others.

I didn't know at the time that I could have bought those
rules in hard-copy form directly from POSIX, but it wouldn't
have mattered anyway. Even if I could have afforded the cost, it
always took a long time to get things shipped to Finland. Hence
my appeal for a version that I could download for free from an ftp
site.

Nobody responded with a source for the POSIX standards,
so I went to Plan B. I tracked down manuals for the Sun Microsystems version of Unix at the university, which was operating a Sun
server. The manuals contained a basic version of the system calls
that was good enough to help me get by. It was possible to look at
the manual pages to see what the system call was supposed to do,
and then set about the task of implementing it from there. The
manual pages didn't say how to do it, they just said what the end
results were. I also gleaned some of the system calls from Andrew

Tanenbaum's book and a few others. Eventually somebody sent me the thick volumes containing the POSIX standards.

But my email message did not go unnoticed. Any knowledgeable person (and only knowledgeable people would be reading the Minix site) could tell that my project would have to be an operating system. Why else would I want the POSIX rules? The message aroused the curiosity of Ari Lemke, a teaching assistant at Helsinki University of Technology (where I would have studied had I not been so interested in studying theory). Ari sent me a nice reply, offering to make a subdirectory on the university's ftp site available for when I would be ready to post my operating system for anyone who might be interested in downloading it.

VII.

Ari Lemke must have been quite an optimist. He created the subdirectory (ftp.funet.fi) long before I had something I wanted to release. I had the password, and everything was set up for me to just log in and upload stuff to it. But it took about four months for me to feel I had anything I was willing to share with the world, or at least with Ari and the few other operating system freaks with whom I had been exchanging email.

My original goal was to create an operating system that I could eventually use as a replacement for Minix. It didn't have to do more than Minix, but it had to do the things in Minix that I cared about, and some other things I cared about, too. For example, not only was the Minix terminal emulation bad, but there was no way of performing the job-control function—putting a program in the background while you're not using it. And memory management was done very simplistically, as it still is in the Mac OS, incidentally.

The way you create an operating system is to find out what the system calls are supposed to do, and then write your own program to implement those system calls in your own way. Generally speaking, there are a couple of hundred system calls. Some of them can represent multiple functions. Others are quite simple. Some of the more fundamental system calls are really complicated and depend on a great deal of infrastructure being there. Take the system calls of "Write" and "Read." You need to create a disk driver in order to write something to disk or read something from disk. Take "Open." You have to create the entire file system layer that parses the names and figures out where on the disk everything is. It took months just to write the "Open" system call. But once it was in place, the same code could be used for other functions.

That's how the early development was done. I was reading the standards from either the Sun OS manual or various books, just picking off system calls one by one and trying to make something that worked. It was really frustrating.

The reason: Because nothing is happening, you can't really see any progress. You can make small test programs that test whatever it is you just added. But that doesn't really accomplish anything. After awhile you get to the point where, instead of just reading through a list of system calls, you give up on that approach. It's getting complete enough that you want to run a real program. The first program you have to run is a shell because, without a shell, it's pretty hard to run anything else. And besides, the shell itself contains many of the system calls you will need. Get it running and you will be able to print out a running list of the system calls you haven't implemented.

In Unix, the shell is kind of the mother of all programs. It's there to start up other binaries. (A binary is a program in the 1's and 0's that a machine reads. Whenever you write a program in a computer language, you then compile the source code and it becomes a binary.) The shell allows you to log on in the first place. Okay, traditionally in a real Unix system the first program you run is called init, but init really needs a lot of infrastructure in order to work. It's kind of a controller for what goes on. But when you don't really have anything that works, there isn't any point to having init.

So instead of starting init, the first thing my kernel did was to start the shell. I had implemented about twenty-five system calls and, as I mentioned, this was the first real program I was trying to run. The shell wasn't something I had written myself. I had downloaded onto a disk a clone of the Bourne Shell, which was one of the original Unix shells. It was available over the Internet as free software, and its name was derived from a bad pun. The guy who wrote the original was named Bourne, so was the clone Bourne-Again Shell—commonly referred to as bash.

When you try and load a real program from disk, invariably there's a bug in the disk driver or in the loader because it doesn't understand what it's reading in. So it prints out a running commentary on what it's doing. It's important because that's how you can find out what is going wrong.

I got to the point where my program was loading the shell and generating a printout of every system call that the shell contained that I hadn't yet implemented. I booted, ran the shell, and it would spit back something like: "system call 512 is not done." Day and night I was looking at printouts of system calls, trying to determine which ones I was doing wrong. But this was much more fun than taking a list of calls and just implementing them. You got to see progress being made.

It was late August or early September when I finally got the shell working. From that point, things got a lot easier.

This was a big deal.

When I got the shell working, I was pretty much immediately able to compile a few other programs. The shell was more complicated than the cp (copy) program, for example, or the 1's (for getting a directory listing) program. Everything you needed had to be there for the shell already, so once the shell was working it went from close to zero to 100 in nothing flat, because all these pieces had been in place. At some point there was enough in place that I experienced a *Let There Be Light* moment, because until then, nothing had really worked.

Yes, I felt a great sense of satisfaction. I think that was particularly important because I hadn't been doing anything that summer except working on the computer. This is not an exaggeration. The April through August period is pretty much the best time of the year in Finland. Folks are sailing in the archipelago, sunning themselves on beaches, sitting in their summer-cottage saunas. But I rarely even knew if it was day or night, weekend or weekday. Those thick black curtains blocked out the near round-the-clock sunshine, and the world. Some days—nights?—I'd roll out of bed directly into the chair at my computer, less than two feet away. Apparently my dad was bugging my mom to make me get a summer job. But she didn't mind: I wasn't bothering her. Sara was a bit annoyed that the phone lines were always tied up when I went online. She could probably write that sentence with a little less diplomacy. It's not an exaggeration to say that I had virtually no contact with the world outside my computer. Okay, maybe once a week a friend would knock on my window and if I wasn't scrolling through important code I would invite him in. (It was always a him—remember, this was before geeks were considered cool.) We would drink tea and maybe watch an hour of MTV in the tiny kitchen. Now that I think of it, yes, I do recall going out for an occasional beer or for some snooker after having my window pounded by someone like Juoko (I call him "Avuton," which means "he who slays dragons," but that's another story). But, in all honesty, nothing else was going on in my life at the time.

And I didn't feel the least bit like some pathetic, pale-skinned, propeller-head loser. The shell was operational, which meant that I had actually built the foundation of a working operating system. And I was having fun.

With the shell working, I started testing its built-in programs. Then I compiled enough new programs to actually do something. I was compiling everything in Minix, but I moved the shell over to a special partition that I had created for the new operating system. Privately I called it Linux.

Honest: I didn't want to ever release it under the name Linux because it was too egotistical. What was the name I reserved for any eventual release? Freax. (Get it? Freaks with the requisite X.) In fact, some of the early make files—the files that describe how to compile the sources—included the word "Freax" for about half a year. But it really didn't matter. At that point I didn't need a name for it because I wasn't releasing it to anybody.

VIII.

From: torvalds@klaava.Helsinki.Fi (Linus Benedict
  Torvalds)
To: Newsgroups: comp.os.inix
Subject: What would you like to see most in minix?
Summary: small poll for my new operating system
Message-ID:
  <1991Aug25.205708.9541@klaava.Helsinki.Fi>

Hello everybody out there using minix—I'm doing a
(free) operating system (just a hobby, won't be big
and professional like gnu) for 386 (486) AT clones.
This has been brewing since april, and is starting
to get ready. I'd like any feedback on things people
like/dislike in minix, as my OS resembles it somewhat
(same physical layout of the file-system (due to practical reasons) among other things).

I've currently ported bash (1.08) and gcc (1.40), and
things seem to work. This implies that I'll get something practical within a few months, and I'd like to
know what features most people would want. Any suggestions are welcome, but I won't promise I'll implement them:-)

Linus (torvalds@kruuna.helsinki.fi)

PS. Yes—it's free of any minix code, and it has a multi-threaded fs. It is NOT portable (uses 386 task switching etc.), and it probably never will support anything other than AT-harddisks, as that's all I have:-(.

The most hard-core operating system enthusiasts among the Minix crowd felt a spark. Not many suggestions about Minix features came my way, but there were other inquiries.

>Tell us more! Does it need a MMU?

Answer: Yes

>How much of it is in C? What difficulties will there be in porting? Nobody will believe you about non-portability;-), and I for one would like to port it to my Amiga.

Answer: It's mostly in C, but most people wouldn't call what I write C. It uses every conceivable feature of the 386 I could find, as it was also a project to teach me about the 386. Some of my "C" files are almost as much assembler as C.

As already mentioned, it uses an MMU, for both paging (not to disk yet) and segmentation. It's the segmentation that makes it REALLY 386-dependent (every task has a 64Mb segment for code & data—max 64 tasks in 4Gb. Anybody who needs more than 64Mb/task—tough cookies).

And I even got a few folks offering to be beta testers.

In the end, it wasn't much of a decision to post it. That was how I was accustomed to exchanging programs. So the only real decision was, at what point am I comfortable to dare show this off to people? Or, phrased more accurately: When is it good enough that I won't have to be ashamed of it?

What I ultimately wanted was to have a compiler and a real environment so that you could create programs in Linux itself, without having to use Minix. But I felt so proud when the gnu shell worked that I was ready to let the world see. Also, I wanted feedback.

By the time the shell worked, I had a few rudimentary binaries I'd compiled for the operating system. You really couldn't do anything, but you could see that it was something resembling Unix. In fact, it worked like a very crippled Unix.

So I just decided I would make it available. I wouldn't tell anybody publicly. Instead, I just informed a handful of people by private email, probably between five and ten people in all, that I had uploaded it to the ftp site. Among them were Bruce Evans of Minix fame and Ari Lemke. I uploaded the sources to Linux itself and a few binaries so that you could start something. I told people what they needed to do in order to try and run this thing. They still had to have Minix installed—the 386 version—and they still had to have the GCC compiler. In fact they had to have *my* version of GCC, so I made that available, too.

There's a protocol for numbering releases. It's psychological. When you think a version is truly ready to be released, you number it version 1.0. But before that, you number the earlier versions to indicate how much work you need to accomplish before getting to 1.0. With that in mind, the operating system I posted to the ftp site was numbered version 0.01. That tells everybody it's not ready for much.

And yes, I remember the date: September 17, 1991.

I don't think more than one or two people ever checked it

out. They had to go to the trouble of installing the special compiler, getting a clean partition so they could use that to boot, compiling my kernel, and then running just the shell. Running the shell was basically all you could do. You could print out the sources, which amounted to just 10,000 lines—that's less than 100 pages of paper if you printed with small font. (Now it's something on the order of 10 million lines.)

One of the main reasons I distributed the operating system was to prove that it wasn't all just hot air, that I had actually done something. On the Internet, talk is cheap. Regardless of what you do, whether it be operating systems or sex, too many people are just faking it in cyberspace. So it's nice, after talking to a lot of people about building an operating system, to be able to say, "See, I actually got something done. I wasn't stringing you along. Here's what I've been doing. . . ."

And Ari Lemke, who insured that it made its way to the ftp site, hated the name Freax. He preferred the other working name I was using—Linux—and named my posting: pub/OS/Linux. I admit that I didn't put up much of a fight. But it was his doing. So I can honestly say I wasn't egotistical, or half-honestly say I wasn't egotistical. But I thought, okay, that's a good name, and I can always blame somebody else for it, which I'm doing now.

As I mentioned, my operating system really wasn't very useful. For one thing, it would crash very easily if you filled up memory or if you did anything nasty. Even if you weren't doing anything nasty, the operating system would crash if you kept it running for any length of time. But it wasn't meant to be run at that stage. It was meant to be looked at. Yes, and admired.

So it wasn't intended to be anything but a specialty for the few people who were interested in creating new operating systems. Very technical people—and even within technical people, a special interest group.

Their reaction was invariably positive, but positive in a kind of "It would be nice if it could also do this" kind of sense, or "It looks cool but it really doesn't work on my computer at all."

I remember one email whose writer said he really liked my operating system, and he went on for at least one paragraph to tell me how nice it was. Then he explained that it had just eaten his hard disk, and that my disk driver was flaky or something. He had lost all the work he had done, but he was still very positive. It was fun to read that kind of email. It was a bug report about something that screwed him up.

That was just the sort of feedback I was looking for. I fixed some bugs, like the one that caused it to lock up when it ran out of memory. And I made the big step of porting the GCC compiler to the operating system, so I could compile small programs. That meant users wouldn't need to load my GCC compiler before running the operating system.

IX.

Do you pine for the days when men were men and wrote their own device
drivers?   —announcement of the posting of Linux version 0.02

Early October saw the release of version 0.02, which
included some fixed bugs and a few additional programs. The following month I released version 0.03.

I probably would have stopped by the end of 1991. I had
done a lot of things I thought were interesting. Everything didn't
really work perfectly, but in a software kind of world I find that
once you solve the fundamental problems of a project, it's easy
to lose interest. And that's what was happening to me. Trying to
debug software is not very engaging. Then two things happened
to keep me going. First, I destroyed my Minix partition by mistake. Second, people kept sending me feedback.

Back then I was booting into Linux but used Minix as the
main development environment. Most of what I was doing under
Linux was reading email and news from the university's computer
via the terminal emulator I had written. The university computer
was constantly busy, so I had written a program that auto-dialed
into it. But in December, I mistakenly auto-dialed my hard disk
instead of my modem. I was trying to auto-dial /dev/tty1, which is
the serial line. But by mistake I auto-dialed /dev/hda1, which is the
hard disk device. The end result was that I inadvertently overwrote
some of the most critical parts of the of the partition where I had
Minix. Yes, that meant I couldn't boot Minix anymore.

That was the point where I had a decision to make: I could
reinstall Minix, or I could bite the bullet and acknowledge that
Linux was good enough that I didn't need Minix. I would write the
programs to compile Linux, under itself, and whenever I felt I

needed Minix I would just add the desired feature to Linux. It's a big conceptual step when you drop the original hosting environment and truly make a program self-hosting, so big that I released the new version as 0.10 in late November. A few weeks later came version 0.11.

That's when there actually started to be a number of people using it and doing things with it. Until then, I had gotten maybe one-line bug fixes. But now, people were sending me new features. I remember going out and upgrading my machine to have 8 mgs of RAM instead of 4 mgs, to accommodate the need for additional memory. I also went out and bought a floating-point coprocessor because people had started asking me if Linux would support their floating-point coprocessors. The extra hardware would enable my computer to perform floating-point math.

I remember that, in December, there was this guy in Germany who only had 2 megabytes of RAM, and he was trying to compile the kernel and he couldn't run GCC because GCC at the time needed more than a megabyte. He asked me if Linux could be compiled with a smaller compiler that wouldn't need as much memory. So I decided that even though I didn't need the particular feature, I would make it happen for him. It's called page-to-disk, and it means that even though someone has only 2 mgs of RAM, he can make it appear to be more by using the disk for memory. This was around Christmas 1991. I remember on December 23rd trying to make the page-to-disk work. By December 24th, it kind of worked but crashed every once in awhile. Then on December 25th, it was done. It was basically the first feature I added to serve somebody else's need.

And I was proud of it.

Not that I mentioned anything about it to my family, as we gathered at my paternal grandmother's (Farmor!) to dine on ham and varieties of herring. Each day, the community of Linux users expanded, and I was receiving email from places that I'd dreamed about visiting, like Australia and the United States. Don't ask me why, but I didn't feel the need to discuss any of this with my parents, sister, or any other relatives. They didn't understand computers. I guess I thought they wouldn't understand what was happening.

As far as they were concerned, I was just tying up the phone lines with my modem. In Helsinki it used to be that you had a flat rate during the night, so I tried to do most of the work at home late at night. But occasionally I tied up the phone all day. I tried to get a second line, but the building that housed my mother's apartment was so old that they didn't have any extra lines and weren't interested in adding new ones. Sara was doing nothing but talking on the phone with her friends at the time. At least that's what it seemed like to me. So we had fights, occasionally. Virtual fights. As she talked to her friends, I would force the modem to start dialing so that she would hear *dee-dee-dee-dee-dee* when I was trying to dial out. It would disturb her but she would know that I really, really needed to read email. I never said I was the world's best older brother.

Page-to-disk was a fairly big thing because it was something Minix had never done. It was included in version 0.12, which was released in the first week of January 1992. Immediately, people started to compare Linux not only to Minix but to Coherent, which was a small Unix clone developed by Mark Williams Company. From the beginning, the act of adding page-to-disk caused Linux to rise above the competition.

That's when Linux took off. Suddenly there were people switching over from Minix to Linux. At the time, Linux didn't do everything Minix did, but it did most of the things people really cared about. And it had this one capability that people really, really cared about: With page-to-disk, you could run bigger programs than you had memory for. It meant that when you ran out of memory you could take an old piece of memory, save it off to disk, remember where you saved it, and reuse that memory for the problem you had to solve. This was a big deal in the opening weeks of 1992.

It was in January that Linux users grew from five, ten,

twenty people—folks who I could email and whose names I knew—to hundreds of unidentifiable people. I didn't know everybody using Linux, and that was fun.

About this time there was a hoax speeding its way on the Internet. Some poor boy named Craig was dying of cancer and a popular chain letter urged you to show your support by sending him a postcard. It turned out to be somebody's idea of a sick joke; I don't think Craig ever really existed, much less suffered from cancer. But the appeal generated millions of postcards. So I was only half-serious when I asked for postcards instead of money from people who used Linux. It was like an oh-God-not-another-email-that-asks-for-postcards joke. In the PC world at the time, there had been a strong tradition of shareware. You downloaded a program and you were supposed to send in something on the order of ten bucks to the writer. I was getting emails from people asking me if I would like them to send me thirty bucks or so. I had to say something.

Looking back, the money would have been useful, I guess. I had amassed something like $5,000 in student loans, and had to shell out about $50 a month to pay off my computer. My other major expenditures were pizza and beer. But Linux was keeping me so preoccupied that I wasn't going out much at the time, maybe once a week at most. I didn't need money for dates although I could have used it for hardware add-ons, but that wasn't necessary. Probably a different son would have asked for money for his program, if only to fork over some rent to his working single mom. It never occurred to me at the time. Sue me.

I was more interested in seeing where people were using Linux. Instead of cash, I preferred postcards. And they poured in—from New Zealand, from Japan, from the Netherlands, from the United States. It was Sara who typically picked up the mail, and she was suddenly impressed that her combative older brother was somehow hearing from new friends so far away. It was her first tip-off that I was doing anything potentially useful during those many hours when I had the phone line engaged. The postcards totaled in the hundreds, and I have no idea what happened to them. They must have disappeared in one of my moves. Avuton calls me "the least nostalgic person" he has ever met.

Actually, I didn't want the money for a variety of reasons. When I originally posted Linux, I felt I was following in the footsteps of centuries of scientists and other academics who built their work on the foundations of others—on the shoulders of giants, in the words of Sir Isaac Newton. Not only was I sharing my work so that others could find it useful, I also wanted feedback (okay, and praise). It didn't make sense to charge people who could potentially help me improve my work. I suppose I would have approached it all differently if I hadn't been raised in Finland, where anyone exhibiting the slightest sign of greediness is viewed with suspicion, if not envy. (This has changed a bit since the days when Nokia phones started making their way into pockets the world over, boosting the bank accounts of numerous Finns.) And, yes, I undoubtedly would have approached the whole no-money thing a lot differently if I had not been brought up under the influence of a diehard academic grandfather and a diehard communist father.

Regardless, I didn't want to sell Linux. And I didn't want to lose control, which meant I didn't want anybody else to sell it, either. I made that clear in the copyright policy I included in the copying file of the first version I had uploaded back in September. Thanks to the Berne Convention in Europe in the 1800s, you own the copyright to anything you create, unless you sell the copyright. As the copyright owner, I got to make up the rules: You can use the operating system for free, as long as you don't sell it, and if you make any changes or improvements you must make them available to everybody in source code (as opposed to binaries, which are inaccessible). If you didn't agree with these rules, you didn't have the right to copy the code or do anything with it.

Think of yourself. You put six months of your life into this thing and you want to make it available and you want to get something out of it, but you don't want people to take advantage of it. I wanted people to be able to see it, and to make changes and improvements to their hearts' content. But I also wanted to make sure that what I got out of it was to see what they were doing. I wanted to always have access to the sources so that if they made improvements I could use those improvements myself. It made sense to me that the way for Linux to develop into the best possible technology was to keep it pure. If money was to get involved, things would get murky. If you don't let money enter the picture, you won't have greedy people.

While I wasn't interested in asking for money for Linux, other people were not shy about requesting donations whenever they gave someone a copy of the operating system they had loaded onto a floppy disk. By February, it was not uncommon for folks to attend Unix users' meetings armed with floppies containing Linux. People started asking me if they could charge, say, five dollars just to cover the cost of the disk and their time. The trouble was, that was a violation of my copyright.

It was time to rethink my Linux-is-not-for-sale stance. By that point, Linux was getting so much online discussion that I felt fairly confident that nobody was going to be in a position to just take it and run with it, which had been my big fear. At least they wouldn't do it without generating a lot of negative reaction. If anybody tried abducting Linux and turning it into a commercial project, there would have been a strong backlash, and a growing community of hacker types who would say "Hey, that's Linux! You can't do that," although not in such polite words.

The momentum had been established: On a daily basis, hackers from around the world were sharing their suggested changes. We were collectively creating the best operating system around, and couldn't possibly veer away from our trajectory. Because of this, and because Linux had become so recognizable, I felt comfortable allowing people to sell it.

But before I make myself sound like Mr. Beneficent, let me mention another critical element of my decision. The fact is, to make Linux usable, I had relied on a lot of tools that had been distributed freely over the Internet—I had hoisted myself up on the shoulders of giants. The most important of these free software programs was the GCC compiler. It had been copyrighted under the General Public License, universally known as the GPL (or the "copyleft"), which was the brainchild of Richard Stallman. Under terms of the GPL, money is not the issue. You can charge a million bucks if somebody's willing to pay it, but you have to make sources available. And the person you give or sell the source to has to have all the rights you have. It's a brilliant device. But unlike many hard-core GPL freaks, who argue that every new software innovation should be opened up to the universe under the general public license, I believe it should be the right of the individual inventor to decide what to do with his or her invention.

So I dumped my old copyright and adopted the GPL, a document that Stallman had written with lawyers looking it over. (Because lawyers were involved, it runs on for pages.)

The new copyright was included in version 0.12, but I remember lying awake at night after releasing it, nervous about what commercial interests would do to the system. Looking back now, it seems ridiculous to have been so worried because the commercial interest was relatively small. Something made me think that I had to be careful. One of my worries was—and still is—that somebody would just take Linux and not honor the copyright. Back then I worried that it would be practically impossible to sue anyone in the United States who broke the copyright. It's still a concern. It's easy to prosecute someone for such violations, but I worry about somebody doing it until they're forced to stop.

And there are nagging fears that companies in places like China won't honor the GPL. Practically nothing in their legal system prevents them from breaking the copyright, and in a real sense it's not worth the trouble to go after people who would try to do something illegal. That's what big software companies and the music industry have tried to do and it hasn't been overwhelmingly successful. My fears are mitigated by reality. Somebody might do it for awhile, but it is the people who actually honor the copyright, who feed back their changes to the kernel and have it improved, who are going to have a leg up. They'll be part of the process of upgrading the kernel. By contrast, people who don't honor the GPL will not be able to take advantage of the upgrades, and their customers will leave them. I hope.

Generally speaking, I view copyrights from two perspectives. Say you have a person who earns $50 a month. Should you expect him or her to pay $250 for software? I don't think it's immoral for that person to illegally copy the software and spend that five months' worth of salary on food. That kind of copyright infringement is morally okay. And it's immoral—not to mention stupid—to go after such a "violator." When it comes to Linux, who cares if an individual doesn't really follow the GPL if they're using the program for their own purposes? It's when somebody goes in for the quick money—that's what I find immoral, whether it happens in the United States or Africa. And even then it's a matter of degree.

Greed is never good.

X.

Minix vs. Linux

The attention wasn't all positive. Although confrontation never has been my best sport, I was bullied into defending Linux and my manhood when Andrew Tanenbaum kept making attacks on the operating system that was supplanting his own. We're nerds, so it was all done via email.

Who could blame him for getting hot under the T-shirt? Before any Linux newsgroups had been created, I routinely used Minix newsgroups to make announcements about Linux or find people who were interested in the operating system. Why should Andrew like that?

So, for starters, he was unhappy about my infringing on his newsgroup. And he obviously wasn't too pleased that his operating system was becoming eclipsed by this new creation from the snowy wilds of Finland—and that so many developers were joining the project. He also had opposing ideas for how operating systems should be built. At the time, Andrew was part of a camp of computer scientists who favored the microkernel approach to operating systems. He had done Minix as a microkernel, and Amoeba, the system he was working on at the time, also involved one.

This was a flourishing movement in the late 1980s and early 1990s. And Linux's success was threatening it. So he kept posting unpleasant little jabs.

The theory behind the microkernel is that operating systems are complicated. So you try to get some of the complexity out by modularizing it a lot. The tenet of the microkernel approach is that the kernel, which is the core of the core of the core, should do as little as possible. Its main function is to communicate. All the different things that the computer offers are services that are available through the microkernel communications channels. In the microkernel approach, you're supposed to split up the problem space so much that none of it is complex.

I thought this was stupid. Yes, it makes every single piece simple. But the interactions make it far more complex than it would be if many of the services were included in the kernel itself, as they are in Linux. Think of your brain. Every single piece is simple, but the interactions between the pieces make for a highly complex system. It's the whole-is-bigger-than-the-parts problem. If you take a problem and split it in half and say that the halves are half as complicated, you're ignoring the fact that you have to add in the complication of communication between the two halves. The theory behind the microkernel was that you split the kernel into fifty independent parts, and each of the parts is a fiftieth of the complexity. But then everybody ignores the fact that the communication among the parts is actually more complicated than the original system was—never mind the fact that the parts are still not trivial.

That's the biggest argument against microkernels. The simplicity you try to reach is a false simplicity.

Linux started out much smaller and much, much simpler. It didn't enforce modularity, so you could do a lot of things more straightforwardly than you ever could with Minix. One of the original problems I had with Minix was that if you had five different programs running at the same time and they all want to read five different files, the tasks would be serialized. In other words, you would have five different processes sending requests to the file system: "Can I please Read From File X?" The file system daemon that handles reading takes one of them and sends it back, then takes the next one and sends it back, and so on.

Under Linux, which is a monolithic kernel, you have five different processes that each do a system call to the kernel. The kernel has to be very careful that they don't get confused with each other, but it very naturally scales up to any number of processes doing whatever they want. It makes Linux much faster and more efficient.

Another problem with Minix was that you got the sources but the licenses didn't allow you to do a lot. Take someone like Bruce Evans, who performed major surgery on Minix and made it much more usable. He couldn't just incorporate his improvements. He was restricted to only making patches. From a practical stand-point that's a complete disaster. He couldn't legally make a bootable image available to people so they could easily upgrade. So users had to take a multiple-step process to even get a usable system, which was horribly impractical.

The only time I ended up communicating with Andrew Tanenbaum was in early 1992. Imagine logging on one blizzardy morning and running across the unedited version of this:

```
From: ast@cs.vu.nl (Andy Tanenbaum)
To: Newsgroups: comp.os.minix
Subject: LINUX is obsolete
Date: 29 Jan 92 12:12:50 GMT


I was in the U.S. for a couple of weeks, so I haven't
commented much on LINUX (not that I would have said
much had I been around), but for what it's worth, I
have a couple of comments now.

As most of you know, for me MINIX is a hobby, some-
thing that I do in the evening when I get bored writ-
ing books and there are no major wars, revolutions,
or senate hearings being televised live on CNN. My
real job is a professor and researcher in the area
of operating systems.

As a result of my occupation, I think I know a bit
about where operating systems are going in the next
decade or so. Two aspects stand out:
```

1. MICROKERNEL VS MONOLITHIC SYSTEM

Most older operating systems are monolithic, that is, the whole operating system is a single a.out file that runs in "kernel mode." This binary contains the process management, memory management, file system and the rest. Examples of such systems are UNIX, MS-DOS, VMS, MVS, OS/360, MULTICS, and many more.

The alternative is a microkernel-based system, in which most of the OS runs as separate processes, mostly outside the kernel. They communicate by message passing. The kernel's job is to handle the message passing, interrupt handling, low-level process management, and possibly the I/O. Examples of this design are the RC4000, Amoeba, Chorus, Mach, and the not-yet-released Windows/NT.

While I could go into a long story here about the relative merits of the two designs, suffice it to say that among the people who actually design operating systems, the debate is essentially over. Microkernels have won. MINIX is a microkernel-based system. The file system and memory management are separate processes, running outside the kernel. The I/O drives are also separate processes. LINUX is a monolithic style system. This is a giant step back into the 1970's.

2. PORTABILITY

MINIX was designed to be reasonably portable, and has been ported from the Intel line to the 680x0 (Atari, Amiga, Macintosh), SPARC, and NS32016. LINUX is tied fairly closely to the 80x86. Not the way to go.

Don't get me wrong, I am not unhappy with LINUX. It will get all the people who want to turn MINIX in BSD UNIX off my back. But in all honesty, I would suggest that people who want a **MODERN** *free* OS look around for a microkernel-based, portable OS, like maybe GNU or something like that.

                    Andy Tanenbaum (ast@cs.vu.nl)

I knew I needed to defend my honor, so I wrote back:

From: torvalds@klaava.Helsinki.FI (Linus Benedict
  Torvalds)
Subject: Re: LINUX is obsolete
Date: 29 Jan 92 23:14:26 GMT
Organization: University of Helsinki

Well, with a subject like this, I'm afraid I'll have to reply. Apologies to minix-users who have heard enough about linux anyway. I'd like to be able to just *ignore the bait* but . . . Time for some serious flamefesting!

In article <12595@star.cs.vu.nl> ast@cs.vu.nl (Andy Tanenbaum) writes:

>I was in the U.S. for a couple of weeks, so I haven't commented much on LINUX (not that

>I would have said much had I been around), but for what it is worth, I have a couple of

>comments now.

>As most of you know, for me MINIX is a hobby, something that I do in the evening when

>I get bored writing books and there are no major wars, revolutions, or senate hearings

>being televised live on CNN. My real job is professor and researcher in the area of

>operating systems.

You use this as an excuse for the limitations of minix? Sorry, but you lose: I've got more excuses than you have, and linux still beats the pants off minix in almost all areas. Not to mention the fact that most of the good code for minix seems to have been written by Bruce Evans.

Re 1: You doing minix as a hobby—look at who makes money off minix, and who gives linux out for free. Then talk about hobbies. Make minix freely available, and one of my biggest gripes with it will disappear. Linux has very much been a hobby (but a serious one; the best type) for me: I get no money for it, and it's not even part of any of my studies in the university. I've done it all on my own time, and on my own machine.

Re 2: Your job is being a professor and researcher: That's one hell of a good excuse for some of the brain damages of minix. I can only hope (and assume) that Amoeba doesn't suck like minix does.

>1. MICROKERNEL VS MONOLITHIC SYSTEM

True, linux is monolithic, and I agree that microkernels are nicer. With a less argumentative subject,
I'd probably have agreed with most of what you said.
From a theoretical (and aesthetical) standpoint,
linux loses. If the GNU kernel had been ready last
spring, I'd not have bothered to even start my project: the fact is that it wasn't and still isn't.
Linux wins heavily on points of being available now.

>MINIX is a microkernel-based system. [deleted, but
not so that you miss the point] LINUX is a monolithic
style system.

If this was the only criterion for the "goodness"
of a kernel, you'd be right. What you don't mention
is that minix doesn't do the microkernel thing very
well, and has problems with real multitasking (in the
kernel). If I had made an OS that had problems with a
multithreading file system, I wouldn't be so fast to
condemn others: in fact, I'd do my damnedest to make
others forget about the fiasco.

[yes, i know there are multithreading hacks for
minix, but they are hacks, and bruce evans tells me
there are lots of race conditions.]

>2. PORTABILITY

  "Portability is for people who cannot write new programs"

                   -me, right now (with tongue in cheek)

The fact is that linux is more portable than minix. What? I hear you say. It's true—but not in the sense that ast means: I made linux as conformant to standards as I knew how (without having any POSIX standard in front of me). Porting things to linux is generally/much/easier than porting them to minix.

I agree that portability is a good thing: but only where it actually has some meaning. There is no idea in trying to make an operating system overly portable: adhering to a portable API is good enough. The very/idea/of an operating system is to use the hardware features, and hide them behind a layer of high-level calls. That is exactly what linux does: it just uses a bigger subset of the 386 features than other kernels seem to do. Of course this makes the kernel proper unportable, but it also makes for a/much/simpler design. An acceptable trade-off, and one that made linux possible in the first place.

I also agree that linux takes the non-portability to an extreme: I got my 386 last January, and linux was partly a project to teach me about it. Many things should have been done more portably if it would have been a real project. I'm not making overly many excuses about it though: it was a design decision, and last april when I started the thing, I didn't think anybody would actually want to use it. I'm happy to report I was wrong, and as my source is freely available, anybody is free to try to port it, even though it won't be easy.

Linus

```
PS> I apologise for sometimes sounding too harsh:
minix is nice enough if you have nothing else. Amoeba
might be nice if you have 5-10 spare 386's lying
around, but I certainly don't. I don't usually get
into flames, but I'm touchy when it comes to linux:)
```

There were a few more installments in this, one of my few flame wars. But you get the point: There were opposing voices, even in the early days. (Or maybe the point is: Be careful when you put yourself out there in an electronic forum. Your typos and errors of grammar will haunt you forever.)

Linus and I leave our families and friends back at the campsite and take an afternoon hike along a clear stream. We're camping at Grover Hot Springs, way up in the Eastern Sierra over the July 4th weekend, at a site that seems to have been lifted from the pages of National Geographic— *"This is a Kodak moment," Linus proclaims, pausing to look out over a wildflower-dusted meadow and the dramatic cliffs that provide the backdrop. We settle at a site along the stream, and I ask him to describe his life during those days when Linux's appeal was spreading far beyond its original family of newsgroup enthusiasts, few of whom Linus had even personally met.*

"It must have felt great," I say. "For years you were toiling away on your own in your bedroom, with little contact with the world outside your CPU. Suddenly you have people from every corner of the planet acknowledging what great work you're doing. You're the center of this growing community that is looking to you to—"

"I don't have a memory of it being a big deal for me," he replies. "I really don't think it was. It was kind of the thing I was thinking about all the time, but mainly because there was always a problem to be solved. In that sense, I was thinking about it a lot, but it was not, emotionally, a big thing. Intellectually, it was something big.

"I liked the fact that there were a lot of people giving me motivation to do this project. I thought I had seen the end of it, a point where it was almost done. But that point never came because people kept giving me more reasons to continue and more brainteasers to worry about. And that kept it interesting. Otherwise, I probably would have just moved

on to another project, because that's how I worked, and that was fun. But I suspect I worried more about my nose or something like that," he says.

A few weeks later we are at the Stanford Shopping Center, where Linus is perplexed over the selection of running shoes from which he can choose. "How many miles do you typically run each week?" asks the salesman. Linus smiles; he hasn't run as much as a mile during the past ten years. Exercise hasn't been a major priority. But in his weaker moments, Linus admits that he would like to shed some of his excess poundage.

"Tove must have convinced you to help me get rid of my pouch," he jokes, patting his gut.

"Tell her that her check never arrived this week," I reply.

Soon we are circling the Stanford campus in search of a legal parking space. After maybe half an hour, we do a few stretches, then we start to run over narrow dirt paths past the campus's dried up lake, into the woods, and in the direction of our goal: the huge hillside satellite dish. We never make it. I set an unfairly swift pace and am surprised that Linus can stick right behind me for about a mile. Then he loses his wind. A few minutes later we spread out on the grass along the lake.

"What was your family's reaction to everything that was happening to Linux?" I ask. "They must have been pretty excited about it."

"I don't think anybody really noticed," he replies. "I won't say that nobody really cared. But I had been doing programming most of my life, and this was not anything different as far as they were concerned."

"Well, you must have said something to your folks. Like if your dad was driving you someplace, didn't you say, 'Hey, you're not going to believe this but you know the stuff I've been doing with my computer? Well, I've got hundreds of people who are using it . . .'"

"No," he answers. "I just didn't feel the need to share this with my family and friends. I never had the feeling that I wanted to push it on people. I remember Lars Wirzenius, around the time I was writing Linux, decided to buy XENIX, SCO's version of Unix, and I think I remember he tried to make excuses, like, 'Don't take this the wrong way.' I personally don't think I ever cared. He eventually switched, but it wasn't *a big deal for me. To me the fact that people used it was nice, and it was wonderful that I got comments back, but at the same time it was not that important. I didn't want to spread the gospel. I was proud of having people use my code, but I don't remember ever having the feeling that I wanted to share that with anybody. And I didn't think it was the most important thing on Earth. I didn't think that I was doing something really important because a hundred people were using my software. It was more like it was fun. And that's how I feel about it today."*

"So you didn't even want to tell your parents and family and friends about it. And you really weren't excited by everything that was happening?" I ask, not masking my disbelief.

He waits a few seconds before responding. "I don't remember if I even had feelings back then."

Linus buys a new car, a BMW Z3, a two-seater convertible that he says defines the word "fun." It is metallic blue, the perfect boy's model-car color. He chose that shade because the vehicle doesn't come in bright yellow, his color of choice. BMW yellow, he explains, "looks like pee." For years he parked his Pontiac as close as possible to the entrance to Transmeta's headquarters in a Santa Clara office park. But the BMW is parked outside his office window, allegedly so it can be in the shade. Now when Linus works on his computer he can admire his new car at the same time.

A little more than a year earlier, we had taken our first trip over the mountain to Santa Cruz in a convertible, a white Mustang I had rented for the occasion. And during that excursion, Linus had made a point of stopping to check out the sports cars parked outside the sauna place and brewery we visited. Now we are heading over the mountain in his own sports car. He smiles as he takes the curves on Route 17.

"You deserve this," I say.

I pull a handful of CDs from the glove compartment.

"Pink Floyd?" I ask. "The Who? Janis Joplin?"

"It's the music I grew up listening to. I never bought music when I was a kid, but we had this around the apartment. I guess my mother was playing it, although I remember she was big on Elvis Costello."

It is Friday afternoon, a sparkling Friday afternoon of California perfection with delights for each of the senses: cobalt skies for the eyes, intense sunshine for the skin, the fragrance of mountain eucalyptus, the sweet taste of pure air, the lull of Pink Floyd on upgraded speakers. Sure, to passing motorists we must have appeared to be some sort of postadolescent cliché, spraying on sunblock and doing the classic rock vocals, but not many cars passed Linus's new BMW Z3.

We park among shoddier vehicles along the side of Highway 1 a bit north of Santa Cruz, and make our way down to a mostly empty beach. We spread out on towels in the warm sun and wait a few minutes before I pull my tape recorder from my backpack. Again, I ask him to describe Linus in those early days.

He draws a box in the sand to represent his bedroom, then indicates the location of his bed and computer. "I would roll out of bed and immediately check my email," he says, moving his finger accordingly. "Some days I don't think I ever left the apartment. I wasn't checking my email just to see who was sending me email. It was more a matter of seeing if a particular problem had been fixed. It was more like, What new exciting issue do we have today? Or, if we had a problem, who had a solution?"

Linus tells me that his social life at the time was "pathetic." Then he figures that sounds too pathetic, so he amends it: "Let's say it was one notch above pathetic."

"I didn't become a total complete recluse," he says, "but even though Linux was happening, I was still as antisocial as I had ever been. You noticed that I never contact people by phone. It's always been true. I never call. Most people who are my friends are the kind of people who contact people, and I'm not. You can imagine what that's like for dating, if you never call the woman. So during that time I had a few friends who just came knocking on my window, wanting to come in for a cup of tea. I don't think anybody could really tell the difference at that time—Oh, he's doing something really big and important and someday he'll change the world. I don't think anybody really thought anything of the sort."

Linus's single regular social event in those days was the weekly Spektrum meeting, where he mingled with other science majors. These social encounters created far more anxiety than anything connected with technology.

"What was I worrying about? Just social life in general. Maybe worry is the wrong word, there was more emotional impact. Just thinking about girls. Linux wasn't that important to me at the time. To some degree, it still isn't. To some degree I can still ignore it.

"In those early years at the university, the social thing was very important. It wasn't as if I worried about my hunchback and people laughing about it. It was more like wanting to have friends and things. One of the reasons I liked Spektrum so much was that it was a framework for being social without having to be social. That was the evening I was social and every other evening I sat in front of the computer. It was much more of an emotional thing than Linux ever was. Linux was never something I got really upset about. I never lost any sleep over Linux.

"The things that I got really upset about, and what still makes me upset, is not the technology per se but the social interactions around it. One of the reasons I got so upset about Andrew Tanenbaum's posting was not so much the technical issues he was raising. If it had been anybody else, I would have just blown it off. The problem was that he was posting it to the mailing list and making me . . . I was concerned about my social standing with those people and he was attacking it.

"One of the things that made Linux good and motivational was the feedback I was getting. It meant that Linux mattered and was a sign of my being in a social group. And I was the leader of the social group. There's no question that was important, more important than even telling my Mom and Dad what I was doing. I was more concerned about the people who were using Linux. I had created a social circle and had the respect of those people. That's not how I thought of it at the time, and it's still not how I think of it. But it must be the most important thing. That's why I reacted so strongly to Andrew Tanenbaum.

The sun begins its descent into the Pacific and it's time to leave the beach. Linus insists that I drive his car home—to see how well it responds—and that we take the long and winding way, Route 9, back to Silicon Valley.

Linus says the flamefest with the Minix creator eventually moved into private email because it had become too nasty to be public. It was quiet for a few months. Then, Tanenbaum emailed Linus to direct him to the five-line ad in the back of Byte magazine for somebody's commercial version of Linux.

"The last email I got from Andrew was him asking me if this is really what I wanted to do, have somebody selling my work. I just sent him an email back saying Yes, and I haven't heard from him since," he says.

Maybe a year later, when Linus was in the Netherlands for his first public speech, he made his way to the university where Tanenbaum taught, hoping to get him to autograph Linus's copy of Operating Systems: Design and Implementation, the book that changed his life. He waited outside his door but Tanenbaum never emerged. The professor was out of town at the time, so they never met.

XI.

The hotel room was only slightly above freezing as I lay in bed, shivering, the night before my first speech. In the Netherlands they don't heat places like they do in Finland, and this drafty room even had huge single-pane windows, as if it were meant to be occupied only in the summer. But the coldness wasn't the only thing keeping me awake on the night of November 4, 1993. I was nervous beyond belief.

Public speaking had always been a rough spot for me. In school they made us give presentations about something we had heavily researched—rats or whatever—and I always found it impossible to do. I would stand up there, unable to talk, and just start giggling. And trust me, I'm not a giggler. It was even uncomfortable when I had to go up to the blackboard to show the class how I figured out a problem.

But there I was in Ede, Netherlands, an hour's train ride from Amsterdam, because I had been invited to be speaker at the tenth anniversary of the Netherlands Unix Users Group. I wanted to prove to myself that I could do this. A year earlier I had been asked to speak before a similar organization in Spain, but declined because my fear of public speaking was greater than my desire to travel. And back then, I really loved to travel. (I still like traveling, but it's not nearly the novelty it was for a kid who had barely been out of Finland. The only places I had ever been were Sweden, where we took a few camping vacations, and Moscow, where we visited my dad when I was about six years old.)

It sort of bothered me that I had blown the chance to visit Spain, so I convinced myself that I would accept the next speaking invitation that came along. But I was having second thoughts as I lay in bed, wondering if I would ever overcome my fear of getting up in front of large groups of people, worrying that I would be unable to open my mouth, or, worse, that I would lapse into giggles before the 400 members of the audience.

That's right, I was a mess.

I told myself the usual stuff. That the audience wants you to succeed, that they wouldn't be there in the first place if they didn't like you, and that I certainly knew the topic: the reasons behind the various technical decisions in the writing of the Linux kernel, the reasons for making it open source. Still, I was unconvinced that the speech would be a success, and my mind chugged along like an unstoppable freight-train engine. I literally was shaking in bed—and the frigid air was the least of it.

The speech? Well, the audience was sympathetic to the obviously frightened soul standing before them, clinging to his PowerPoint slides (thank God for Microsoft) like a life preserver, and then haltingly answering their questions. Actually, the question-and-answer session was the best part. After my speech—such as it was—Marshall Kirk McKusik, who was instrumental in BSD Unix, came up to me and told me he found my speech interesting. I was so grateful for the gesture, I felt like getting down on my knees and kissing his feet. There are few people I look up to in computers, and Kirk is one of them. It's because he was so nice to me after that first speech.

My first speech was like shock treatment. So were the ones that followed. But they started making me more self-confident.

David keeps asking me how my stature at the university changed as Linux grew bigger. But I wasn't aware of any professors even mentioning it, or any other students pointing me out to their friends. Nothing like that. People around me at the university knew about Linux, but actually most of the hackers involved in it were from outside of Finland.

In the fall of 1992 I had been made a teaching assistant for Swedish-language classes in the Computer Sciences department. (Here's how that happened: They needed Swedish speaking TA's for the basic computer courses. There were only two Swedish-speaking computer science majors who had started at the university a few years earlier: Lars and Linus. There wasn't much of a choice.) At first I was afraid to even go up to the blackboard and work on problems, but it didn't take long for me to just concentrate on the material and not worry about embarrassing myself. By the way, three years later I was promoted to research assistant, which meant that instead of getting paid for teaching I was paid to work in the computer lab, which mostly meant doing development work on Linux. It was the start of a trend: having someone else pay me to do Linux. That's basically what happens at Transmeta.

David: "So when did it start becoming a big deal?"

Me: "It's still not a big deal."

Okay, I'll amend that. It started becoming more of a deal when it became clear how many people depend on Linux as something other than a toy operating system. When they started using it for more than just tinkering around, I realized that if something goes wrong, I'm responsible. Or at least I started feeling responsible. (I still do.) During 1992 the operating system graduated from being mostly a game to something that had become integral to people's lives, their livelihoods, commerce.

The shift occurred in the spring of 1992, about a year after I had started terminal emulation, when the first version of the X windowing system ran under Linux. That meant the operating system was capable of supporting a graphical user interface and that users could work in multiple windows simultaneously, thanks to the X windowing project, which had its origins at MIT. It was a big change. I remember that I had joked with Lars about it, around a year before it actually happened, telling him that someday we would run X and be able to do it all. I never thought it would happen that quickly. A hacker named Orest Zborowski was able to port X to Linux.

The way the X window system works is by way of the X server, which does all the graphics. The server talks to the clients, which are the things that say "I want a window and I want it this big." The communication goes through a layer called sockets, or, more formally, Unix Domain Sockets. It's how you communicate internally in Unix, but you also use sockets to communicate over the Internet. So Orest wrote the first socket layer for Linux just to port X to it. Orest's socket interface was kind of tacked on and not integrated with the other code. It was a situation in which I agreed to the patch because we needed it, even though it was fairly raw.

It took me awhile to get used to the notion that we had a graphical user interface. I don't think I even used it on a daily basis for the first year or so. And these days I can't live without it. There are always a ton of windows up when I work.

Orest's contribution not only enabled us to have windows, but it also opened a big door for the future. The domain sockets were used for the local networking that enables the X windowing system to operate. We could build on those same sockets to enable Linux to make the major leap to external networking—to have the ability to link computers. Without networking, Linux was usable only for people who sat at home and used a modem to dial up somewhere, or who did everything locally. With great optimism, we started developing Linux networking on top of those original sockets, even though they hadn't been meant for networking at all.

I was so confident that we could easily do it that I made a leap in the version-numbering scheme. In March 1992 I had planned to release version 0.13. Instead, with the graphical user interface in place, I felt confident that we were maybe 95 percent of the way to our goal of releasing a full-fledged, reliable operating system, and one with networking. So I named the new release version 0.95.

Boy, was I premature. Not to mention clueless.

Networking is nasty business, and it ended up taking almost exactly two years to get it right, to a form where it could be released. When you add networking you suddenly introduce a host of new issues. There are security issues. You don't know who's out there and what they want to do. You have to be really careful that people don't crash your machine by sending it bad junk packets. You're not in control of who's trying to contact your machine anymore. Also, a lot of people have very different setups. With TCP/IP the networking standard, it's difficult to get all the time-outs right. It felt as if the process would drag on forever. By the end of 1993 we had an almost usable networking capability, although some people had serious problems getting it to work. We couldn't handle networks that didn't have 8-bit boundaries.

Because I had been overly optimistic in the naming of version 0.95, I was caught in a bind. Over the course of the two years it took to get version 1.0 out the door, we were forced to do some crazy things with numbers. There aren't many numbers between 95 and 100, but we continually released new versions based on bug fixes or added functions. By the time we got to version 0.99, we had to start adding numbers to indicate patch levels, and then we relied on the alphabet. At one point we had version 0.99, patch level 15A. Then version 0.99, patch level 15B, and so on. We made it all the way to patch level 15Z. Patch level 16 became version 1.0, the point where it was usable. This was released in March 1994 with great fanfare at the University of Helsinki Computer Sciences Department auditorium.

The period leading up to it had been kind of chaotic, but nothing could put a dent in Linux's popularity. We had our own Internet newsgroup, comp.os.linux, which grew out of the ashes of my flamefest with Andrew Tanenbaum. And it was attracting hordes. Back then the Internet Cabal, the folks who more or less ran the Internet, kept unofficial monthly statistics on how many readers each newsgroup attracted. They weren't reliable statistics, but they were the best information available on the popularity of your site—in this case, how many people were interested in Linux. Of all the newsgroups, alt.sex was the perennial favorite. (Not my particular favorite. Although I did check it out once or twice to see what the fuss was about, I was pretty much your typical under-sexed nerd, more eager to play with my floating point processor than to keep abreast of the latest reports from the sexuality front—newly discovered lovemaking positions or reports from heavy petters or whatever else it was that so many people were talking about on alt.sex.)

With the Cabal's monthly statistics, I could easily track the popularity of comp.os.linux. And trust me, I kept track. (While I might be somebody's idea of a folk hero, I've never been the selfless, ego-free, techno-lovechild the hallucinating press insists I am.) By the fall of 1992, the estimates for our newsgroup were on the order of tens of thousands of people. That many people followed the newsgroup to see what was going on, but they weren't all using Linux. Every month, when the statistics came out, there was a summary report of the forty most popular newsgroups. If your newsgroup didn't make it to the top forty, you could fetch the full report on other newsgroups' popularity from a special maintenance newsgroup. Usually I had to go find the full report.

The Linux newsgroup kept creeping up the chart. At one point it made the top forty and I was happy. That was pretty cool. I seem to remember having written a fairly gloating article to comp.os.linux in which I basically listed the various os (operating system) newsgroups, including Minix, and said, "Hey look at this, we're more popular than Windows." Remember that, back then, people who liked Windows were not on the Internet. We made it to the top five sometime in 1993. I went to bed that night brimming with self-satisfaction, excited by the fact that Linux had become almost as popular as sex.

There certainly was no such matchup in my own little corner of the world. I truly did not have a life. By this time, as I mentioned earlier, Peter Anvin had organized an online collection that generated $3,000 in donations to help me pay off my computer, which I did at the end of 1993. And for Christmas, I upgraded to a

486 DX266, which I used for many years. But this was my life: I ate. I slept. Maybe I went to university. I coded. I read a lot of email. I was kind of aware of friends getting laid more, but that was okay.

Quite frankly, most of my friends were losers, too.

XII.

The speech in Ede almost convinced me that I could survive anything, even something as terrifying as standing up before a group of total strangers and being the focus of their attention. My confidence was slowly building in other areas, too. I was being forced to make quick decisions regarding Linux fixes and upgrades, and with each decision I felt increasingly comfortable in my role as leader of a growing community. The technical decisions had never been a problem; the problem was figuring out how to tell one person that I preferred another's suggested changes—and being diplomatic about it. Sometimes it was as simple as saying, "So-and-so's fixes are working fine. Why don't we just go with those?"

I never saw the point of accepting anything other than what I thought was the best technical solution being presented. It was a way of keeping from taking sides when two or more programmers offered competing patches. Also, although I didn't think of it this way at the time, it was a way of getting people to trust me. And the trust compounds. When people trust you, they take your advice.

Of course you have to establish a foundation for all the trust. I guess that started not so much when I wrote the Linux kernel as when I posted it to the Internet, opening it up to anyone who wanted to join in and add the functions and details they liked, with me making ultimate decisions regarding the guts of the operating system.

Just as I never planned for Linux to have a life outside my own computer, I also never planned to be the leader. It just happened by default. At some point a core group of five developers started generating most of the activity in the key areas of development. It made sense for them to serve as the filters and hold the responsibility for maintaining those areas.

I did learn fairly early that the best and most effective way to lead is by letting people do things because they *want* to do them, not because you want them to. The best leaders also know when they are wrong, and are capable of pulling themselves out. And the best leaders enable others to make decisions for them.

Let me rephrase that. Much of Linux's success can be attributed to my own personality flaws: 1) I'm lazy; and 2) I like to get credit for the work of others. Otherwise the Linux development model, if that's what people are calling it, would still be limited to daily email messages among a half-dozen geeks, as opposed to an intricate web of hundreds of thousands of participants relying on mailing lists and developers' conventions and corporate sponsorship in maybe 4,000 projects that are taking place at any one time. At the top, arbitrating disputes over the operating system's kernel, is a leader whose instinct is, and has always been, not to lead.

And things work out for the best. I divested myself of things that didn't hold much interest for me. The first of these was the user level, the external parts of the system that end users deal with directly, as opposed to the deep-down, internal code. First somebody volunteers to maintain it. Then the process for maintaining all the subsystems becomes organic. People know who has been active and who they can trust, and it just happens. No voting. No orders. No recounts.

If two people are maintaining similar kinds of software drivers, for example, I'll sometimes accept the work from both of them and see which one ends up getting used. Users tend to lean on one versus the other. Or, if you let both maintainers work it out, they may end up evolving in different directions and their contributions end up having very distinct uses.

What astonishes so many people is that the open source model actually works.

I guess it helps to understand the mentality of hackers in the free software universe. (By the way, I usually try to avoid the term "hacker." In personal conversations with technical people, I would probably call myself a hacker. But lately the term has come to mean something else: underage kids who have nothing better to do than sit around electronically breaking into corporate data centers, when they should be out volunteering at their local libraries or, at the very least, getting themselves laid.)

The hackers—programmers—working on Linux and other open source projects forego sleep, Stairmaster workouts, their kids' Little League games, and yes, occasionally, sex, because they love programming. And they love being part of a global collaborative effort—Linux is the world's largest collaborative project—dedicated to building the best and most beautiful technology that is available to anyone who wants it. It's that simple. And it's fun.

Okay, I'm starting to sound like a press release with all this shameless self-promotion. Open source hackers aren't the high-tech counterparts of Mother Teresa. They do get their names associated with their contributions in the form of the "credit list" or "history file" that is attached to each project. The most prolific contributors attract the attention of employers who troll the code, hoping to spot, and hire, top programmers. Hackers are also motivated, in large part, by the esteem they can gain in the eyes of their peers by making solid contributions. It's a significant motivating factor. Everybody wants to impress their peers, improve their reputation, elevate their social status. Open source development gives programmers the chance.

Needless to say, I was spending most of the year 1993 like I had spent most of 1992, 1991, et cetera: hunched over a computer. That was about to change.

Following in the academic footsteps of my grandfather, I was a teaching assistant at the University of Helsinki, assigned to the fall semester of the Swedish-language "Introduction to Computer Sciences" course. That's how I met Tove. She had more of an impact on my life than even Andrew Tanenbaum's book, *Operating Systems:*

Design and Implementation. But I won't bore you with too many details.

Tove was one of fifteen students in my course. She had already received a degree in preschool education. She wanted to study computers, too, but wasn't progressing as quickly as the rest of the class. She eventually caught up.

The course was so basic—this was the fall of 1993, before the popularity of the Internet—my homework assignment for the class one day was to send me email. It sounds absurd today, but I said: "For homework, send me email."

Other students' emails contained simple test messages, or unmemorable notes about the class.

Tove asked me out for a date.

I married the first woman to approach me electronically.

Our first date never ended. Tove was a preschool teacher and six-time Finnish karate champion who had emerged from a functional family, although that's how I'd describe any family that was not as quirky as mine. She had a lot of friends. She felt like the right woman for me from the very first moment we got together. (I'll spare you the elaboration.) Within a few months Randi the cat and I had moved into her minuscule apartment.

For the first two weeks, I didn't even bother bringing over my computer. Not counting my army service, those two weeks were the longest span of time that I had been away from a computer since I had been eleven years old and sitting on my grandfather's lap. Not to dwell on this, but it still holds the record for being my biggest stretch—as a civilian—without a CPU. Somehow. I managed (again, the details aren't interesting). My mother, the few times I saw her then, would mutter something about "a triumph of Mother Nature." I think my sister and father were just stunned.

Soon, Tove went out and got a cat to keep Randi company. Then we settled into a nice pattern of spending evenings alone or with friends, waking up at 5 A.M. so she could get to her job and I could go to the university early, before anyone would be there to disturb me, and read my Linux email.

King of the BALL

I.

The birth of version 1.0 meant something new for Linux: the need for public relations. I would have been just as happy to introduce the new version to the world pretty much the way I had introduced previous versions. I would write something on the newsgroup like "Version 1.0 is out. Deal with it." (Okay, not in those exact words.)

A lot of other people thought it was much more of a big deal. They wanted version 1.0 for marketing purposes. There were all these budding commercial companies that had started to sell Linux. To them, version 1.0 was important for psychological, not technical, reasons. I couldn't disagree. The fact is, it looks bad when you try and sell version 0.96 of an operating system.

I wanted it out because it was a milestone for me, and because it meant I could stop fixing bugs for awhile and go back to development. The companies and the Linux community wanted to foist it onto the public in a major way.

We needed a public relations strategy. I wasn't going to personally champion the effort. I wasn't interested in putting out press releases or making statements. Others thought it should be done that way, so others volunteered to pick up the torch. This was pretty much how Linux itself was done—and somehow, it all actually worked.

Lars was one of the driving forces behind making that first official release a real event. He and a few others thought the university would be the most appropriate place to make the announcement. It made sense. My bedroom was too small. And it would have set a wrong precedent to host the announcement at a commercial site. So Lars volunteered to coordinate the event with the university. The computer sciences department at the University of Helsinki was small enough that he could just talk to the head of the department.

The University of Helsinki was more than happy to offer up the main auditorium of the computer sciences department for the introduction of Linux Version 1.0. And why not? How often does a university have anything worthy of television news?

I did agree to give a talk. But it bore none of the horror of my Ede experience. Okay, some things *were* harder, now that I think about it.

Like having my dad in the audience. And the fact that it was on Finnish TV. It was the first time I ever got the chance to see myself on television. Both of my parents were in the audience (but I'm fairly certain they weren't sitting together). Tove was there, too. It was the first time my dad met Tove, so for me it was more than just the announcement of Version 1.0. Since I was involved in the last-minute speech preparations, like making sure my slides were okay, I wasn't there when they actually met. That apparently happened when they were walking into the auditorium. Maybe I caught it out of the corner of my eye.

In that talk, and in virtually every other one over the next several years, I spoke not so much about the technology but about Open Source. It was nice. It changed some opinions about Linux inside the computer science department. Before that, Linux was something the computer science department was proud of, and mildly encouraged. But after the announcement, people within the department started taking Linux more seriously. After all, they had seen it on the news.

Over the years, some have suggested that the university was trying to take credit for Linux. That wasn't the case. The department had always been very supportive. They even gave me a job that enabled me to work on Linux on their time. And that was in the early days, so nobody was saying, " 'Let's push this because some day it will be world famous." But at the same time they were pleased to be a big part of the announcement. It provided great public relations. I know there are now more Swedish-speaking students in the computer sciences department, which had always been overshadowed by the Polytechnic University.

Success envy is considered a Finnish cultural characteristic. And as Linux became better known in the world at large, I got a lot of questions about whether I had problems with people at the university being envious of me. The opposite turned out to be true; they were very supportive. Early on they started getting rid of X terminals and installing PCs with Linux instead.

The announcement launched Linux into the above-the-radar zone in Finland, and it started generating publicity elsewhere, too. A lot of the early headlines came about because some journalist had stumbled over Linux and got excited about it. From a business standpoint, Version 1.0 was never very challenging to any of the big players. Linux was getting the market that Minix and Coherent had. But there was little attention outside that community, which was fine. It was far more attention than I had expected initially.

Regardless, journalists, mostly from trade publications, started knocking at my door—literally. It didn't make Tove happy to wake up on a Saturday morning to find a Japanese reporter bearing gifts—usually watches, as they probably heard somewhere that I have a thing for them—and wanting to do an interview. It made her even less happy when I would invite them in. (It was a pattern I would repeat for years, until we made our new house a Journalist-Free Zone. In my least considerate moments, I would even forget to tell Tove that I had invited a journalist to our house for an interview—and I would forget, too. The reporter would show up and Tove would have to entertain him or her until I made it home.) Then there were the fan websites that started popping up, such as the one based in France that primarily consists of a much-updated gallery of embarrassing photos of me. Like the one of me from a Spektrum meeting: I'm shirtless, drinking a beer, looking studly.

Not.

And it wasn't only journalists or Linux hacker types who were showing an interest. Suddenly, people with big expense accounts wanted to talk to me about their technology. Unix had long been seen as an operating system with vast potential, mostly because of its power and multitasking capabilities. So corporations that were interested in Unix started keeping an eye on Linux. One of those was the networking company Novell, which had started a skunkworks project based on Linux. It was a Unix desktop they evolved called Looking Glass. It looked nice, but it was up against a wall: It lacked the standard of the time, which was the Common Desktop Environment.

In August 1994, they said they would pay me to visit them in Orem, Utah, to talk to them about their desktop. Novell was offering me my big chance to see America, so I told them I would accept if they would pay for me to visit another U.S. city. Even as an unworldly Finn I kind of suspected that Orem—and even Salt Lake City—weren't quite representative of the rest of the country. They suggested Washington, D.C., but I didn't want to go there. I figured it would be just like any other capital. They suggested New York, but I thought it would be more interesting to go to California.

Inside Novell's headquarters, it was hard to determine just how serious people were about the project. (In the end, they ended up being not very serious at all; they eventually killed the project, and the nine people involved started up Caldera.) But I was getting my first taste of the United States, where I somehow figured I would live at some point in my life. Novell's commitment to Linux notwithstanding, the United States seemed to be the center of the growing technology universe.

My visit to the United States was a bit of a jolt. The first thing that struck me was how new everything was, compared to Europe. The Mormon Church had had its 150th anniversary a few years before my visit, so they had cleaned up the main temple. It was shining white. Coming from Europe, where all the churches are old and have the patina of time, I could only think of one thing when I saw the white temple: Disneyland. It looked like a fairy-tale castle, not a church. And in Orem I made the mistake of checking out the hotel's sauna. It was one of those porta-potty saunas, literally made of plastic, and it was barely hotter inside than outside. I came away from it thinking they can't do saunas in the United States and feeling a little homesick.

And I started learning the ropes. Just as visitors to Finland learn quickly not to start up conversations with random strangers in bars, I learned that in Utah—and, I later learned, the rest of America—you cannot rationally discuss the subject of abortion or rifles. There's a 50-percent chance that you'll get somebody who's very emotional about those issues, and it's easy to get into a big fight about something that shouldn't be fought about. People don't get hung up about those issues in Europe. The reason people get so defensive about their own positions in the United States is that they've heard the other position so much. There are probably more rifles per capita in Finland than in many other places, but they're mostly used for hunting. It's not a big thing.

Another thing I quickly learned during my first days on U.S. soil: Root beer sucks.*

After Utah, I flew to San Francisco and really, really liked it. I spent so much time walking around the city that I developed a major case of sunburn and had to remain indoors for an entire day.

I remember walking across the Golden Gate Bridge, looking up at the Marin Headlands, excited about the possibility of hiking in those hills as soon as I crossed the bridge. But by the time I made it to the Marin side, I had lost all interest in walking anymore. I could never have predicted that six years later, almost to the day, I would be sitting at the crest of those windy Headlands,

---

*Boy, that has to be an acquired taste. I'm guessing it started out with Puritans who couldn't drink beer because it has alcohol. So they concocted a beverage that didn't have alcohol in it and happened to be made with roots, and they called it "root beer" to fool people into thinking it was good stuff. And after ten generations of people being fooled into thinking it was good stuff, people bought into it. Today, Americans like root beer because they have ten generations of genetic engineering behind them.

looking out on the Pacific Ocean, San Francisco Bay, the bridge, the fog, and San Francisco itself, explaining all this to David's tape recorder.

It would take only a year for me to return to the United States. I came back to speak at DECUS, (Digital's User Group) in New Orleans. There were only forty people at the meeting, so it wasn't a terrible ordeal. Best of all, that's when I met Maddog, a.k.a. Jon Hall. He was a technical marketing person for Digital Unix and an old-time Unix user. He was responsible for sending me over for the talk. Maddog, who is known for his chest-length beard and his absurd sense of humor (not to mention his propensity to snore), heads Linux International, an organization that works to support Linux and Linux users. He's also a godfather of my daughter Patricia.

Another legacy of that New Orleans meeting: Maddog arranged for Digital to lend me an Alpha. That's how Linux got ported to something other than a PC. Before that time, people had ported Linux to other architectures. There was a port to a 68K, the Motorola 68000 machines used by Atari and Amiga. But in those cases Linux didn't work on both platforms at the same time. To make that version of scaling work, you rip out the pieces that don't work on the new platform and you write new pieces. But the Alpha was the first real port of Linux. Basically the same sources worked on both the PC and Alpha. You add an abstraction layer so that the same code gets compiled in two different ways to work on two different architectures. It's still the same code, but it ends up working on different architectures.

When we released Version 1.2 in March 1995, the kernel had grown to include 250,000 lines of code, the new magazine *Linux Journal* claimed a 10,000-reader circulation, and Linux was capable of running on Intel, Digital, and Sun SPARC processors. That was a big step.

II.

It's 1995 and there is a host of growing commercial versions, and Linux companies are attracting a strong following. The university has elevated me from a teaching assistant to a research assistant, which means more money and less time teaching. I'm slowly—very slowly—completing the coursework for my master's degree, which is about porting Linux to different architectures. Tove has introduced me to squash, and we have a weekly game; we're fairly evenly matched.

From this bliss, a problem emerges. It turns out that an opportunistic fellow from Boston has registered the trademark for the word Linux. Not only that, but he sent email to the *Linux Journal* and a few other Linux companies asking for 5 percent of their revenues as a "thank you" for the trademark.

When I heard about this, I felt a twinge of *déjà vu*. The guy's name sounded familiar. I checked my email archives and saw that maybe a year and a half earlier he had sent me an unsolicited email in which he first asked me if I believed in God, and then said he had a tremendous business opportunity for me. This was before spamming became a global obsession, the innocent years before anyone thought to pollute the Internet with offers of get-rich-quick schemes. No, I hadn't bothered responding to the fellow's email, but because it was so unusual for its time, I saved it.

So we had a little crisis on our hands. We were hackers. Nobody thought about checking the trademark register.

The guy wasn't a professional trademark squatter. He apparently just did it this one time. Trademarks come in different categories, and he registered his in the computer category. You have to submit evidence with your trademark application, so he gave the trademark office a disk on which he claimed to have a program called Linux.

There was some panic. Everybody in the Linux community knew we would contest the trademark. The problem was, we didn't have an organization for putting up a good fight. There wasn't even enough money to hire a lawyer. None of the companies felt comfortable about laying down the required amount, which was $15,000. (Today they go through that in a month's worth of Mountain Dew.) But at the time, it was a considerable amount of money for a single company. So *Linux Journal* and some other companies decided to pump money into Linux International, which would fight the trademark. Linux International had been started in Australia by a person named Patrick D'Cruze who migrated to the United States in 1994 to help promote Linux worldwide. The year of the trademark dispute was the year when Maddog became its executive director. Everybody trusted him, and still does.

I was in Finland, trying to beat Tove in squash or to beat Avuton in snooker, and I had no interest in getting involved in this. I just wanted the entire nightmare to go away. My preference at the time was to just get rid of the trademark, to get it declared invalid because of prior use in the industry. We had enough paperwork to show that Linux had, in fact, a history of prior use. The trouble was, our lawyer convinced us that it would be a wasted effort, that we should not even try to get Linux declared a public domain instead of a trademark. The only way for it to really be in the public domain, he explained, was for it to become generic. And Linux at the time wasn't that generic. The trademark office probably wouldn't even consider it to be generic today. We could lose the battle, he said. Or if we invalidated the old trademark, somebody could possibly come along and trademark it anew.

The solution he suggested was to transfer the trademark to somebody else. My vote went to Linux International, but there was a lot of opposition to that. Linux International was young and unproven. People were worried about Linux International being taken over by commercial interests. (It hasn't happened, I might add.) There was also strong concern about who would eventually take over for Maddog if he were to step down.

So all eyes looked to me. The lawyer suggested that the legal arguments would be easier if the Linux trademark were to be transferred to me because I was the original user of the word. That's the strategy we took. We reached an out-of-court settlement because that seemed like the easiest and cheapest thing to do. Like most out-of-court settlements, the details can't be discussed. Not that I even know them. I was happily uninterested in it all.

When I went back to check my original email from the guy, I realized that it had nothing to do with patents. It was obvious that he just wanted to talk to me. Maybe he tried to contact me to get me to pay him. Or maybe, if I had shown myself to be a true believer and soul brother in his faith, he would have just *given* me the trademark. I don't know.

I accept the fact that some people are not morally all there. But what was more irritating at the time was the fact that the entire trademark system put this onus on me, who had done nothing wrong, to go out and fight the guy.

As a result of the messy squirmish, I hold the Linux trademark. What that means is, when companies like VA Linux file for an IPO, their prospectus has to mention the fact that the company doesn't even own the trademark for half of its name. (In that particular case, the company was involved in the legal process of getting approval from me to use the word Linux.) But I've gotten accustomed to that sort of thing.

The trademark episode was just an unexpected growing pain for Linux. And a distraction. But no sooner was it settled then another surfaced: An engineer at Intel's research lab in Portland, Oregon, said his company was using Linux in its exploration of new architectures. He asked me if I wanted to move there for a six-month internship.

Tove and I had spoken in vague terms about possibly living in the United States. She knew how much I had enjoyed my few visits there, root beer notwithstanding. We agreed that the opportunities—not to mention the climate—were better in America. (By the way, I am totally convinced that the U.S. system of motivating employees is far more realistic, and produces better results, than the European model. In Finland if a worker is much better than his colleagues, you give him just a little more money and keep it very quiet. In America, you give him a lot more money—and it works.) The internship seemed like a great way of testing the waters, or, since it was in the Pacific Northwest, the rainwaters, and we agreed that I should pursue the opportunity. But I was ambivalent. I felt a bit uneasy about leaving school without having finished my master's. Something inside me, possibly the memory of my professor grandfather, didn't take to the notion of being a dropout. In the end, my feelings didn't even matter. The engineer's manager decided that it would be difficult for me to obtain the required six-month work permit from the U.S. Immigration and Naturalization Service for the internship.

So we stayed in Helsinki. By the time Finland's legendary revelers were toasting the arrival of New Year's Day, 1996, I was inching toward the master's degree finish line. I only needed to complete one small course to finish the credit requirements. And I also had to write my thesis. Ironically, it would be the first time I got any academic credit for my work on Linux, which had consumed most of my life throughout my college years.

The year 1996 brought with it a wake-up call. In egalitarian Finland, you get a state-mandated seniority raise after you've been at a job for three years. When I saw my first pay stub reflecting the new salary, I felt a jolt: I had been working at the university long enough to be given seniority. Would I spend my entire working career there? Was I destined to become my grandfather? Remember my description of him from earlier in this book: bald, overweight, and not smelling like anything. I started checking myself in the mirror with some regularity. My hairline was creeping back a couple of millimeters. Extra kilos seemed to have made their way to my once-skinny torso. I was twenty-six and for the first time in my life I was feeling old. I had been at the university for going on seven years; I knew I could graduate fairly quickly if I got my act together.

My ten-year-old daughter Kaley thinks it's the apex of super-stardom to have someone buy you a penguin. We are sitting around a campfire on a clear Sierra night when Linus explains that a Linux user group in Bristol, England, bought him a penguin. Kaley cannot imagine that he hasn't bothered to visit the creature. Then he elaborates: Actually, they didn't buy him a penguin, but instead sponsored one in his name. And the sponsorship lasts for a year, he thinks.

The Torvalds family is trying to understand the concept behind 'smores. Somebody looks up from his roasted marshmallow and makes the mistake of asking how the penguin came about as the planetary symbol of Linux in the first place.

"The penguin was my idea," says Tove. "Linus was trying to find a symbol for Linux because people were asking, 'Shouldn't there be a symbol?' He was thinking of things he'd seen. The Linux companies had their own symbols. One of the companies had a pink triangle as its symbol. But I knew that was the international symbol for gays, so I told him that had already been taken. He said he would like to have something nice, something sympathetic.

I thought about penguins. Linus had been bitten by a fairy penguin at a zoo in Australia. He likes to pet things. He's always poking at stuff like rattlesnakes. Those penguins at the zoo were about one foot high, and he just reached into the cage to pet one of them. He kind of played with his fingers as if they were fish. The penguin came at him, bit him, noticed he was not a fish. He got bitten by a penguin but he liked it

138

*anyway. I got the feeling he was sold on penguins after that. He wanted
to see penguins wherever it was possible.*

*"So when he started looking for a symbol I said, 'Why don't you
have a penguin because you fell in love with those penguins?' He said,
'Okay, I'll think about it.' "*

*Here's where Linus, sitting maybe three bodies away from Tove,
shakes his head.*

"No, it was not her idea," he says. "She's wrong."

*This was a departure. Linus and Tove don't make a habit of
disagreeing. Tove is astounding in her ability to deftly handle the
responsibilities of the girls and the household—and a famous husband—
fending off journalists with her karate skills. Linus seems downright
cheerful about chipping in by occasionally folding laundry or doing his
morning chore of making the cappuccino. Even during the stress of a ten-
hour car trip with the on-again-off-again needs of a pair of young kids,
Linus and Tove handle it all smoothly: Think of the marital equivalent
of a well-crafted Scandinavian sofa bed.*

We found the kink.

*The story, according to Linus, is that while Tove may in fact have
vaguely mentioned penguins at some early stage, it was in a conversation
with two high-ranking Linux types that the icy creatures were first seriously considered as the operating system's official mascot.*

*Tove has her take on this version. "He thought it wasn't a good
idea after all, because it was* my *idea. He went on thinking about a
possible symbol. Then we were in Boston with Maddog and Henry Hall.
They started talking about the symbol. I said to them, 'What about a
penguin. Do you think it's nice?' They said yes. I think that made
Linus think it might be a good idea after all."*

*"Henry Hall said he knew an artist who could draw it for him,
but that never happened. The next thing I knew, Linus had asked on the
Internet if there were people who wanted to send in pictures of penguins."
He chose a version by Larry Ewing, a graphic artist who works at the
Institute for Scientific Computing at Texas A&M University.*

But this wasn't to be just any penguin. Above all, Linus wanted one that looked happy, as if it had just polished off a pitcher of beer and then had the best sex of its life. Even beyond that stipulation, he wanted one that was distinct. Hence, while all other penguins have black beaks and feet, those features are orange on the Linux mascot, making it look almost like a penguin whose father was a duck. As if Daffy Duck got a little kwazy on a cruise to Antarctica and had a wild one-night-stand with some native fowl.

III.

News of my decision to work for Transmeta Corporation was greeted with the same reaction in the Linux community as was the news that Tove and I had figured out how to conceive a child and were expecting one at the end of 1996.

When word leaked out in the spring that Tove was pregnant, the more vocal among Linux user newsgroup participants wanted to know how I planned on balancing the demands of Linux maintenance with those of a family. A few months later, when it became known that I would (finally) be leaving the University of Helsinki to work for the secretive Transmeta in Silicon Valley, the big, worldly debate centered on whether I could possibly keep true to my open source philosophy in a dreaded commercial environment, as opposed to a neutral academic institution. Transmeta was partly funded by Microsoft cofounder Paul Allen, folks declared in protest; some claimed it must be an elaborate scam for taking control of Linux.

I'm not saying those aren't valid concerns for loyal members of the Linux community, but it's just . . . gimme a break! The fact is, neither the birth of Patricia in December 1996 (and Daniela sixteen months later and Celeste forty-eight months later) nor my job at Transmeta, which began in February 1997, has caused the downfall of Linux. I felt all along that if anything were to negatively affect my work with Linux, I would have taken the obvious necessary step of turning it all over to somebody I trust.

But I'm getting ahead of myself.

In the spring of 1996, just as the weather was breaking, I finished the last of my required coursework for my master's. It was about this time that I heard from Peter Anvin, the Linux community member who three years earlier had organized the online collection that helped me pay off my first PC. Like everybody else who prowled the Linux newsgroups, he knew I would soon be graduating. He had been working at Transmeta for about a year, and approached his boss to explain that he knew this guy in Finland who might be good for the company. He came to meet with me briefly while he was visiting his mother in Sweden. He talked up Transmeta, which was pretty hard to do since it was in stealth mode and he couldn't tell me much of anything. The rumor among programmers was only that it was involved in developing "programmable chips." At the very least it was great to meet Peter in person.

A week after he returned to California, he sent me an email asking when I could come. This was hugely different from the experience I had had with Intel a year earlier, when an engineer wanted to hire me for an internship but it never happened because of the paperwork issues.

It would be fun just to get a trip to California, I thought.

This was the first job interview of my life. I didn't have a CV. I didn't know what Transmeta was doing; it was in a strange land.

I was more worried about the implications of moving to the United States than about getting the job itself, so I didn't even think of my meetings as being interviews. What mattered more, it seemed, was to learn what these guys were up to. It was a fairly strange interview situation.

After the first day, I went back to my hotel across the street from Transmeta's office-park headquarters. In my jet-lagged state I thought it was all interesting, but I also thought that the folks at Transmeta were crazy. At that point the company didn't have any silicon at all. No hardware. Everything was done with a simulator, and the demonstration of the simulation booting into Windows 3.11 and running solitaire did little to convince me that anything was going to happen. After that first day I wondered if it wasn't all a waste. I distinctly remember thinking: Maybe this isn't going to turn out—either as a technological innovation for Transmeta or a job for me.

I literally slept on it. Actually, it wasn't much of a sleep. I lay in bed thinking about Transmeta's plans. Then I started fantasizing about having a backyard palm tree. Then I started ruminating over what I had seen on the simulator. It was a memorable, fitful night, but nothing like the frostbitten anxiety of Ede.

By morning, I was somewhat excited. By the end of the second day, I was very excited. That's when the stress began.

Before accepting Transmeta's offer, I talked it over with various people. When word got out that I was considering the job, I received a number of other offers. In Finland I got an offer from Tele, which was using Linux in some capacity. Through Maddog I got an offer at Digital. (No offense, but Boston in winter isn't a whole lot better than Helsinki in winter. Okay, maybe it is.) I talked to some of the Red Hat people. They offered me a job and said they would pay better than Transmeta was paying, even though they had no idea what the poposed salary was because I hadn't even discussed money with the company. The Red Hat crowd said they would even top Transmeta's stock options, whatever they would be. But I wasn't interested in working for any particular Linux company—even one that was fortunate enough to be located in the middle of North Carolina.

In the end, I got five job offers without ever formally looking for a job. Transmeta's was the most exciting, by far.

I said yes. It felt weird. The next thing I did was tell the university I would be leaving. *That's* when the stress really began. For me, it was a giant step that meant there was no turning back. We were having a new child, moving to a new country, and I was leaving the safe nest of the University of Helsinki—but first I had to write my thesis. In retrospect, I guess getting all those changes over at once was a good idea. But it was madness.

There was no formal announcement (why should there be?).

Just word circulating on the Internet, and the aforementioned debate about whether I would be able to remain true to Linux and free software in the evil corporate environment, and between the changing of diapers. Back then, people had this view of Linux as something that was mainly developed by university students, not settled-down people. I guess it was understandable that they would be nervous.

I wrote my thesis over a long weekend and turned it in minutes before taking Tove to the hospital to deliver Patricia, who was born forty hours later. That was December 5th, 1996. Being a father seemed like the most natural thing in the world.

The next several weeks we were busy with Patricia and constantly worrying about obtaining the approvals for our U.S. visa paperwork, which was taking forever. We figured it would help if we were married, so sometime in January—I always have to ask Tove the date—we went to a government office to be officially wed. We had three guests: Tove's parents and my mother. (My dad was in Moscow). It was a strange time. At some point we shipped most of our belongings to the United States without knowing when we would be able to fly out. To say good-bye to all of our friends, we hosted a housecooling party, the reverse of a housewarming. Twenty people crammed into the small, recently emptied one-bedroom apartment. In good Finnish tradition, everybody got drunk.

Our visas finally arrived and on February 17, 1997, we boarded a morning flight to San Francisco. I remember the temperature in Helsinki: 0 degrees Fahrenheit. I remember Tove's family at the airport, crying when we said good-bye—they're very close. I don't remember if my family was there or not. They must have been. Or maybe not.

We landed in the United States and made our way through customs carrying a baby and two cats. Peter Anvin was there to greet us as we rented a car for the drive down to Santa Clara, to the apartment complex we had chosen during an apartment-hunting trip we had taken a few months earlier. It all felt surreal, particularly the 70-degree difference in climate from Finland.

Our belongings wouldn't arrive for another two months. We spent the first night sleeping on an air mattress we had brought with us. The next day we went out to buy a real bed. Until our furniture made it to California, Patricia had to sleep in her carriage. It was something that really annoyed Tove, although David points out that it is sort of cyclical, referring to the first three months of my life that were spent in a laundry basket. We didn't do much cooking (we still don't) and didn't know where to go for dinner. We ate most of our meals either at the food court of a local shopping mall or at a fast-food place. I remember telling Tove we had to find some new places to eat.

With the move and getting accustomed to the new job at Transmeta, I didn't have a lot of time to devote to Linux during those first couple of months. The new job occupied much of my time and my after-work hours were spent with Tove and Patricia, trying to get to know the new area. It was a fairly busy time. We had absolutely no money. I had this great salary, but everything went toward getting furniture. Buying our cars was a hassle because we had no way of establishing a credit history. We even endured hassles proving we were capable of paying for telephone service.

My computer was on a ship that was inching its way around the Horn of Africa. It was the first period of time when I was quiet on the Web, and my absence worried a lot of people. It was like, Okay, now he's working for a commercial company. . . .

Many people asked outright: Does this mean Linux will die off as a free system? I explained that under my agreement with Transmeta I could continue doing Linux. And that I wasn't going to go away. (I couldn't think of a way to say that I was just catching my breath.)

Life in Transmetaland.

One of the problems with explaining to people how the move to the States and into the commercial world wasn't going to change me was the fact that Transmeta was just about the most secretive company around. There was only one rule concerning what you could talk about, and that rule was very simple: "Say nothing." Which just made Linux people sometimes wonder what kind of strange cult I had joined, and whether I was ever coming back. I couldn't even tell my mother what I was up to—not that she would have been interested.

What I was doing at Transmeta wasn't all that strange. The first thing I actually ended up doing was fixing some of the Linux problems that Transmeta had. The company was using a lot of multiprocessor Linux machines. I had never personally worked on the Linux SMP (Symmetric MultiProcessing) issues, and it turned out that many things didn't really work the way they were supposed to. I took this as a personal affront, and had to fix it, of course.

But my real work was actually being part of the Transmeta softball team.

Oh, I mean soft*ware* team. We didn't play all that much softball. None of the Silicon Valley leagues would let us join unless we agreed to tell them what we were up to.

I don't know how familiar people are with Transmeta. As I'm typing this, we're actually in our silent period before the (please, God, buy our stock) IPO, and we're no longer secret, although we're back in our stealth mode due to SEC rules about initial public offerings. Let's hope that by the time this book is out, everybody and his dog has heard about Transmeta and bought (*subliminal message*: STOCK) one or more of our CPUs. Because that's what Transmeta does—CPU's. Hardware.

But Transmeta does more than just hardware. Which is just as well because, quite frankly, I wouldn't know a transistor from a diode even if one kicked me in the head. What Transmeta does is *simple* hardware that relies on clever software to make a simple CPU look like much more than it really is—like a standard Intel-compatible ×86, in fact. And with the hardware being made smaller and simpler, the CPU ends up having fewer transistors, which in turn makes it use less power, which as everybody realizes will become increasingly more important in a mobile world. This clever software is why Transmeta has a rather large software team, and why I was there.

This all fit me quite well. A non-Linux company that did something that was technically quite interesting (understatement of the year—I still don't know of another company that has ever seriously even tried to do what Transmeta does). And it was in an area that I knew intimately: low-level programming of the quite esoteric 80×86 family of CPU's. As you undoubtedly recall, it was the act of getting to know that CPU in the first personal computer I owned that had started the whole Linux project in the first place.

The fact that Transmeta wasn't a Linux company was also important to me. Don't get me wrong: I loved fixing Linux problems at Transmeta, and I've been involved in several internal projects about Linux. (In fact, these days it's probably impossible to find a serious technology company without such projects.) But at Transmeta, Linux was secondary—which was just what I wanted. I could continue to do Linux, but I didn't feel I would have to make the technical compromises that would favor the company's goals over Linux itself. I could continue to think of Linux as a hobby in which only technology mattered, and nothing else held sway over my decisions.

So during the day, I worked for Transmeta. I wrote and maintained the "×86 interpreter" that we still use today (although others maintain it now). The interpreter is basically the piece of Transmeta software that looks at Intel instructions one at a time, and executes them (i.e., it "interprets" the language of the 80×86 architecture, one instruction at a time). I ended up doing other things later, but that's how I got into the strange and wonderful world of hardware emulation.

During the night, I slept.

My deal with Tramsmeta was clear: I had been given vague assurances that I could work on Linux during work hours too. Trust me, I took full advantage of that.

A lot of people believe in working long days and doing double, triple, or even quadruple shifts. I'm not one of them. Neither Transmeta nor Linux has ever gotten in the way of a good night's sleep. In fact, if you want to know the honest truth, I'm a firm believer in sleep. Some people think that's just being lazy, but I want to throw my pillow at them. I have a perfectly good excuse, and I'm standing by it: You may lose a few hours of your productive daytime if you sleep, oh, say, ten hours a day, but those few hours when you *are* awake you're alert, and your brain functions on all six cylinders. Or four, or whatever.

IV.

Welcome to Silicon Valley. One of the first things I got to do upon landing in this strange galaxy was to meet the stars.

I received an email from Steve Jobs's secretary about how he'd like to meet me and could I spare an hour or two. Not knowing what it was all about, I said sure.

The meeting was at Apple's headquarters on Infinity Loop Drive. It was with Jobs and his chief technical guy, Avie Tevanian. This was when Apple was starting work on OS X, the Unix-based operating system that wasn't released until September 2000. There wasn't much formality to the meeting. Basically, Jobs started off by trying to tell me that on the desktop there were just two players, Microsoft and Apple, and that he thought that the best thing I could do for Linux was to get in bed with Apple and try to get the open source people behind Mac OS X.

I stuck around because I wanted to learn about the new operating system. It's based on Mach, the microkernel developed at Carnegie Mellon University. In the mid-1990s the Mach was expected to be the ultimate operating system, and a lot of people were interested in it. In fact, IBM and Apple used Mach as the basis for their ill-fated Taligent joint-venture operating system.

Jobs made a big point of the fact that Mach's low-level kernel is open source. He sort of played down the flaw in the setup: Who cares if the basic operating system, the real low-core stuff, is open source if you then have the Mac layer on top, which is not open source?

He had no way of knowing that my personal opinion of Mach is not very high. Frankly, I think it's a piece of crap. It contains all the design mistakes you can make, and managed to even make up a few of its own. One of the arguments against microkernels has always been performance. So a lot of people did research projects aimed at determining how to turn microkernels into something that performs really well. All of the resulting recommendations made it into Mach. As a result, it became a very complicated system with rules of its own. And it *still* doesn't perform that well.

Avie Tevanian had been one of the Mach people when it was a university project. It was kind of interesting, discussing what he and Steve saw as the issues. At the same time, we disagreed fairly fundamentally on technical matters. I really didn't think there was a reason for open source or Linux people to get involved. Sure, I could understand why they wanted to get more open source developers into their system; they were seeing the momentum build behind Linux. But I don't think they were seeing it quite enough. I don't think Jobs realized that Linux would potentially have more users than Apple, although it's a very different user base. And I don't think Steve would be quite as eager to dismiss Linux as a desktop system today as he was three years ago.

I explained why I didn't like Mach. For understandable reasons that didn't go over very well. They'd certainly heard the arguments before. Obviously, I was very set on Linux and Tevanian was very set on Mach. It was interesting to see how they discussed some of the technical issues. One of the immediate problems I could see involved how they planned on supporting old Mac applications in the new operating system. They wanted to do all the old stuff with a compatibility layer. All the old Mac applications would run within one new tacked-on process. But one of the major shortcomings of the old Mac is the lack of memory protection, and this solution does nothing to solve that problem. Only the new Mac applications would have memory protection. It didn't make sense to me.

We had basic differences in how we viewed the world. Steve was Steve, exactly as the press portrays him. He was interested in his own goals, and especially the marketing side. I was interested in the technical side, and not very interested in either his goals or his arguments. His main argument was that if I wanted to get the desktop market I should come join forces with Apple. My reaction was: Why should I care? Why would I be interested in the Apple story? I didn't think there was anything interesting in Apple. And my goal in life was not to take over the desktop market. (Sure, it's going to happen, but it's never been my goal.)

He didn't use very many arguments. He just basically took it for granted that I would be interested. He was clueless, unable to imagine that there could be entire segments of the human race who weren't the least bit concerned about increasing the Mac's market share. I think he was truly surprised at how little I cared about how big a market the Mac had—or how big a market Microsoft has. And I can't blame him for not knowing in advance how much I dislike Mach.

But even though I disagreed with almost everything he said, I kind of liked him.

Then there was the first time I met Bill Joy. I walked out on him.

Okay, to be fair, I didn't realize who he was when I first met him. It was at the Jini preview. Jini is Sun Microsystems' interaction agent language, an extension to Java. It's for doing seamless networking between completely different systems. You could have a printer that was Jini-aware, and anything on the same network that spoke Jini would be able to use Jini automatically.

Sun Microsystems had invited me and about a dozen other open source people and technical people to a private preannouncement briefing that would take place in a hotel room in downtown San Jose during Java World. The reason we were invited: They were doing Jini under what, at Sun Microystems, passes for open source.

When I went there, I kind of knew Bill Joy was there. He

had been the key person behind BSD Unix and later joined Sun as chief scientist. I had never met him before. He just came up to me and said he was Bill Joy and I kind of didn't react to it. I hadn't come there to meet him but to see what Sun thought about open source and how they were going to enter open source. A few minutes later, Bill himself was explaining the reasons for making it open source and they had a limited demonstration of the system.

Then they started explaining their licensing. It was horrible. Just stupid. Basically it boiled down to the fact that if somebody else wanted to use the system in even a half-commercial way, it wouldn't be open source at all. I thought it was a completely idiotic idea. I was really upset about the fact that, on the invitation, they had touted their open-sourceness. It was open source in the sense that you could read the source, but if you wanted to make any modifications or make it part of your infrastructure, you had to license it from Sun. If somebody at Red Hat wanted to make the latest Red Hat CD version of Linux Jini-aware, the company would have to license the Jini technology from Sun.

I asked a few questions to see if I had understood it correctly. Then I walked out on them.

I was just so pissed off that they had gotten people there by claiming open-sourceness that after I found out what it was all about I literally said, "Forget it, I'm not interested," and left.

My understanding was that they wanted me there simply to inform me and that maybe if I had been enthusiastic they would have liked a press quote or something. That plan backfired. But maybe they will learn. Apparently people later convinced them to open source their Star Office. So I guess it all just takes time.

I'm told that they continued the meeting that day and had dinner, and that everybody else stayed.

The second time I met Bill Joy turned out to be a much better experience. About a year and a half later he invited me out for sushi.

His secretary phoned me to set up a time. Bill lives and works in Colorado and apparently spends one week out of each month in Silicon Valley. We went to Fuki Sushi in Palo Alto. It's one of the better sushi places in the Valley. Of course it's nothing like Blowfish Sushi in San Francisco, with its nonstop Japanese animations to look at, or Tokyo Go Go in the Mission, with its hip crowd, or Sushi Ran in Sausalito, with its important patrons, or Seto Sushi in Sunnyvale, which has the best spicy tuna sushi of them all.

Okay, we were at Fuki Sushi, and it was kind of fun because Bill was trying to get real wasabi. I didn't know this at the time, but in most Japanese restaurants in the United States, what passes for wasabi is actually just colored horseradish. It turns out the wasabi plant lives only in Japanese streams and is difficult to grow commercially. Bill tried to explain this to the waitress and she really didn't get the concept. She was Japanese, but she thought that wasabi was wasabi. He asked her to ask the chefs.

The back-and-forth was sort of funny. This was a social dinner. He basically made it clear that if I wanted to work for Sun I could just give him the word and he would make something happen. But that was not the main thing. It was more of an opportunity to talk about the issues. He started reminiscing about how he'd been the maintainer of BSD Unix for five years and how he had grown to appreciate having the commercial side around him through Sun. He talked about how important it was to have the kind of commercial support that a company like Sun could provide. I found it fun and interesting to hear him talk about the early days of Unix. It didn't make one bit of difference to me that we were never able to taste genuine wasabi. I distinctly remember thinking he was probably the nicest and most interesting of the high-profile people I had met in Silicon Valley.

Flash forward three years. I pick up *Wired* magazine only to encounter his horribly negative article about technology entitled "The Future Doesn't Need Us." I was kind of disappointed. Obviously, the future doesn't need us. But he didn't have to be so negative about it.

I don't want to tear apart his article line by line, but I have a general belief that the saddest thing that could ever happen to humanity would be that we would just go on and on, as opposed to evolving. Bill seemed to feel that advances like genetic modification make us lose our humanity. Everybody always thinks that something different is inhuman because right now we *are* human. But as we continue to evolve with whatever happens, in 10,000 years we will not be human according to today's standards. We will just be a different form of human.

In Bill's article, he seemed afraid of that. My feeling is that it's unnatural—and fruitless—to try and curb evolution. Instead of trying to find two different kinds of dog to produce the desired offspring, obviously we will resort to genetics; it seems inevitable that this will happen for people, too. In my opinion, changing the human race through genetics is preferable to leaving the status quo. I think that, in the bigger picture, it would be a hell of a lot more interesting to ensure the continued evolution of not just humans but of society, in whatever direction it goes. You can't stop technology, and you can't stop the advances we make in our knowledge of how our universe works and how humans are designed. It's all moving so fast that some people, like Bill Joy, find it scary. But I see it as part of our natural evolution.

I disagree with Joy about how we should deal with the future the same way I disagreed with his notion of open source. I disagreed with Steve Jobs about technology. It sounds like I spent my first years in Silicon Valley being disagreeable, but that's not true. I was doing a lot of coding and taking Patricia to the petting zoo and in general broadening my horizons—like learning the awful truth about wasabi.

V.

Our overnight success.

Do you ever read advocacy newsgroups? The entire purpose of their existence is to advocate something, which means to put something else down. So if you go on them you find nothing but "My system is better than your system" nonsense. It's its own form of online masturbation.

The reason I mention advocacy newsgroups is that, despite their absurdity, they do offer a clue to what is happening. So when corporations first decided that Linux was the darling of operating systems, the growing commercial support wasn't discussed first in the press or at the checkout counter at Fry's Electronics, but on advocacy newsgroups.

Let me back up. In the spring of 1998, a third blonde entered my world: Daniela Yolanda Torvalds got produced on April 16th, making her the first Torvalds to be a U.S. citizen. She and Patricia are sixteen months apart, the same as Sara and me. But I guarantee they won't be as embattled as my sister and I were growing up—certainly not with Tove's moderating influence. Or her karate skills.

Two weeks before Daniela's birth, the open source community—which had until recently been called the free software community—got its biggest boost ever. That's when Netscape opened up the source code for its browser technology in a project named Mozilla. On the one hand, the news got everyone on the newsgroups excited because it raised the visibility of open source. But it also made a lot of people, including me, fairly nervous. Netscape was in trouble at the time, thanks in large part to Microsoft, and the opening up of its browser was seen as a somewhat desperate measure. (Ironically, the browser's roots were in open source. It began as a project at the University of Illinois.)

People on the newsgroups were expressing their fears that Netscape would muck things up and give open source a bad name. Now there would be two big-name open source projects— Netscape and Linux—and the reasoning was that if Netscape, the better known of the two, were to fail, the reputation would impact Linux, too.

And to a large degree, Netscape did fail. The company had trouble getting open source developers interested in the project for the longest time. It was just a huge body of code and the only people who could get into that code were Netscape people.

The project was somewhat doomed not only because of its size but also, because Netscape wasn't able to make everything available as open source—only the development version, which was fairly broken at the time the company released it. The company couldn't GPL the browser because not all the code was theirs—the Java portion was licensed from Sun, for example. Not everyone on the newsgroups agreed with Netscape's license. On the whole, the license was fairly mellow, but if you're someone like Richard Stallman you don't like mellow.

I thought it was wonderful that Netscape took this step, but I didn't view it as a personal achievement. I remember that Eric Raymond took it really personally. He was extremely happy about it. His paper, "The Cathedral and the Bazaar," which did an excellent job of explaining the open source philosophy and history, had been released the year before and was cited as one of the reasons behind the Netscape decision. He was actively pushing open source. He had been at Netscape on a number of occasions, trying to convince them to open up their browser. I was there only once. In fact, Eric had visited a number of companies bearing the open source message. I was interested in the technology, not the evangelization.

Within 24 hours of Mozilla being released, an Australian team that called itself the Mozilla Crypto Group created the cryptography module. Back then, non-U.S. citizens were prohibited from using encryption generated on U.S. soil. Suddenly, somebody from Australia had done the work, so non-U.S. citizens were in a position to use it. But there was a catch. Given the export restrictions of the time, the Mozilla project couldn't take the Australian code. If it made its way to the United States, it couldn't be re-exported. This meant that one of the first successes of the great Netscape experiment couldn't become part of Mozilla.

We were all worried because Netscape had received a lot of news coverage. And for that first year, people walked on eggshells. Nobody wanted to say anything negative about Netscape for fear that it would result in bad press for open source and scare other companies away.

But two months after Netscape's move, Sun Microsystems joined the game by declaring that it would become the first major hardware vendor to join Linux International. It would support Linux on its servers. The company with the unimpressive licensing scheme for its Jini project had decided that Linux was worth taking seriously. The newsgroups overflowed with self-congratulations. With Sun on board, Linux developments made their way from Internet discussions to the trade press. Outsiders were suddenly interested, but mostly technical outsiders.

Then came IBM.

IBM has been known for being fairly stodgy, so everybody was taken by surprise when the company announced in June that it would sell and support Apache, the most popular commercial Linux version used for Web servers. You could run Apache on AIX, IBM's UNIX, and that's probably what a lot of people who bought IBM did. That's how Apache got to IBM's attention. Somebody must have noticed that most of those server machines ended up using Apache, so they calculated that they would sell more servers if they had the in-house expertise to support such customers. Or maybe they were acting on feedback from customers who said they would buy IBM machines but would run Apache.

It's relatively easy to install Linux on a computer. But for most companies, one of the big issues, historically, has been: Who do we blame when something goes wrong? Obviously, there are the Linux companies like Red Hat that provide the support, but it was a psychological advantage for customers to know that IBM would be there for them. When IBM started getting into open source, a lot of people suspected it was just lip service. But that turned out not to be the case. IBM dipped its toes in the water by running and supporting Linux on its server boxes and then sort of waded all the way in. Next came the small PC servers. Then, the regular PCs. Then, the laptops. The company has announced it will spend $1 billion on Linux this year.

IBM did a lot of its Linux work on its own. I think one of the reasons they liked Linux was because they could just do what they wanted to do without having to deal with licensing issues. It's a company that has had its share of hassles. IBM was screwed over by Microsoft after the two companies jointly developed the OS/2 operating system, which turned out to be just Windows on steroids. Microsoft failed to support OS/2 because it wasn't interested in sharing the market. Windows NT is what came out of it from the Microsoft side. But OS/2 never paid back to IBM the billions of dollars poured into it. And IBM was plagued with the licensing issues over Java. I think they were just happy not to have all that aggravation with Linux.

There's no doubt that IBM was Linux's biggest coup. And it generated only excitement on the newsgroups—not the sort of paranoia provoked by the Netscape announcement, or any of the seething anticommercialism that has periodically (okay: frequently) divided Linux enthusiasts.

By July, Informix announced that it would port its databases to Linux, meaning that even if you used Linux to operate your computer, you could run an Informix database. It wasn't such a big deal at the time. The company had been having financial trouble, but it was still one of the top three database vendors. Linux people were mildly happy about the development, and were writing self-congratulatory essays in Linux advocacy groups.

Within weeks, from out of nowhere, Oracle followed suit. Oracle dominated databases. Long before the announcement there had been rumors (on the newsgroups) about the company having some internal ports to Linux. And, since Oracle is synonymous with Unix servers, it wasn't such a major leap to Linux. But if you followed the newsgroups, we had definitely entered the big time. The Oracle announcement had a huge psychological impact, even if its technical impact was zero.

Like the IBM announcement before it, Oracle's big move was felt not only by the Linux community but by the folks who are commonly referred to as management decision-makers, although some people prefer the term "suits." No longer would they be able to say that they couldn't use Linux because their business depends on databases.

While the news was gratifying, it didn't change my life. Tove and I were juggling two adorable kids. Most of my nonfamily hours were spent on Linux maintenance, both at home and in the office. To keep from favoring any one version of Linux, I used Red Hat at work and SuSE, a European version, at home. At one point I felt I wasn't getting enough exercise, so I decided to ride my bicycle the six miles between our apartment and Transmeta's headquarters. It was on a Monday. There were no hills to climb, but a strong wind blew in the wrong direction, making it more challenging than I wanted. By the time I left work ten hours later, the wind had shifted so that it was still in the wrong direction. I phoned Tove and she picked me up. Needless to say, biking-to-work didn't happen again.

I add this innocuous detail only to illustrate that the Linux developments weren't affecting my daily life. Most of the activity was taking place at corporations. Technical people, who had long known about Linux were being approached by their companies' leaders who had been seeing articles about Linux in the trade press, or hearing about it. They would ask their technical folks what the fuss was all about. Then, once they learned the benefits, they would make the decision to have their servers run Linux.

The situation was playing out in information-technology departments throughout the world, although most of it took place in the United States. It was rarely a decision based on the non-cost of Linux, because the software itself actually represents a small part of such an investment. The service and support are much more costly. What tended to sway the suits were the simple technical arguments: Linux was stronger than the competition, which consisted of Windows NT and the various flavors of Unix. And, importantly, people just hate having to do things the way Microsoft or anybody else says they have to do them. You can do things with Linux that you can't do with the competition. The original people who used Linux did so because they could get access to sources in ways they couldn't with commercial software.

From that perspective, things hadn't changed much since I had released Version 0.01 from my bedroom. Linux was more flexible than other systems out there. You got to be your own boss. And, at least in the case of Web servers, it didn't contain the "bloat"—the many unnecessary features—that make up competing operating systems.

Another thing Linux had in its favor: Despite its growing popularity as an operating system for Web servers, it really didn't occupy a niche. This is important as a way of understanding Linux's success.

Mainframe computers were a niche. Unix in general was a series of niches—the U.S. Department of Defense super-computer niche, the banking niche. The folks selling operating systems for mainframes and other big systems made money because they were charging a lot for their operating systems. Then Microsoft came along and charged ninety bucks. Microsoft didn't go after the banking niche or any other niche, but suddenly it was everywhere.

It was like getting invaded by locusts. It's hard to get rid of that kind of invasion. (Not that locusts are bad. I like all animals.)

It's a lot better to be everywhere and take over every niche, and that's what Microsoft did. Think of a fluid organism that flows into any place it can find. If one niche is lost, it's not a big deal. The organism surrounds the world, flowing into anything that's interested.

The same thing is happening with Linux today. It flows into anything that's interested. Linux doesn't have just one niche. It's small and flexible and finds its way into many places. You find it in supercomputers, at important places like the U.S. Government's Fermilabs, or NASA. But that's kind of an outflowing of the server space. Which is an outflowing of the desktop space—which is where I got started. And at the same time you'll find Linux in embedded devices, everything from antilock brakes to watches.

Watch it flow.

Meanwhile, there's a great advantage to grass roots. The best and the brightest of the next generation are using your product because you are the thing that makes that generation excited. In an earlier generation, it wasn't so much Microsoft and DOS but PCs that got people excited. If you were into PCs, you were into DOS. There wasn't much choice.

And that was a huge advantage for spreading Microsoft.

If you look at the brightest young kids around, they're not *all* doing Linux, but a lot of them are. Sure, one of the reasons that the open source philosophy and Linux both have major followings in universities is simple: the antiestablishment sentiment. (The same antiestablishment sentiment that made such a huge impact on my dad's life.) It's the Big, Evil Microsoft Corporation & Wicked, Greedy, Too-Fucking-Rich Bill Gates vs. the We're-In-It-for-the-Love-and-Free-Software-for-Everybody & the Self-Effacing (Seeming) Folk Hero Linus B. Torvalds thing. Those kids graduate and take jobs in corporations, where they bring with them their love for Linux.

So folks who've ventured into the depths of Microsoft tell

me they've seen my face on dartboards. My only comment: How could anybody possibly miss my nose?

But I'm getting ahead of myself. IBM's big announcement in the spring of 1998 was followed by similar announcements by every major hardware vendor. By August, *Forbes* magazine had "discovered" our little world by putting a picture of me on the cover with the words, "Peace, Love, Software." As company after company made an (inevitable) commitment to Linux, you no longer had to peruse the advocacy newsgroups to read the tea leaves.

VI.

Linux had captured the planet's heart like some improbable Olympic gold medalist from an unrecognizable third-world nation.

I was the poster boy. In a press interview, Eric Raymond explained that part of my appeal (or whatever) was that I was "less visibly odd than a lot of other hackers." Okay. That's one hacker's opinion. Not everybody liked the situation. Richard Stallman campaigned to change the name Linux to gnu/Linux, using the logic that I had relied on the GNU gcc compiler and other free software tools and applications to get Linux off the ground. Others were growing increasingly irritated by the fact that Linux was finding a home in the corporate realm.

The press was playing up the dichotomy between the Idealists and the Pragmatists (not my terms!) among Linux's now hundreds of thousands of participants. Under that division, those who feared that Linux's ideals were incompatible with the goals of capitalism were dubbed the idealists. I led the pragmatists. But I saw such analysis as journalistic nonsense—a simplistic attempt to fit everything neatly into a world of black vs. white. (I have the same problem with the way folks view the Linux phenomenon as a Linux vs. Microsoft war, when in fact it's something else entirely, something far more wide-reaching. It's a more organic way of spreading technology, knowledge, wealth, and having fun than the world of commerce has ever known.)

To me, it was a non-issue. Without commercial interests,

how else would Linux flow into new markets? How else would it create opportunities for innovations? How else would it be able to reach the people who want an alternative—a free alternative—to the bad technology that's out there? What more realistic way for open source to take hold than through the sponsorship of corporations? And what better way of getting some of the less interesting work accomplished, boring stuff like maintenance and support, than doing it inside companies?

Open source is about letting everybody play. Why should business, which fuels so much of society's technological advancement, be excluded—provided that they play by the rules? Open source can do nothing but improve the technology that companies create, and maybe make them less greedy.

And even if we wanted to stop the forces of commercialism, what could we do? I was not willing to suggest we hide, go underground, refuse to talk to commercial people.

Anticommercial sentiments have always been a part of the open source community, but it wasn't until Linux became a household word among low-tech households that there was a lot at stake. The newsgroups were aflame with the paranoid rantings of some of the vocal crazies. None of the Linux developers I interacted with were worried at all. But others raged on about how Red Hat or some other company would pervert the notions of open source, and about how some people were losing their idealism.

To some degree, it's probably true that some open source folks stood to get diverted from their idealism. But while certain people saw that as a losing proposition, I felt that it simply gave us more choice. Technical people who were worried about things like feeding their kids now had an option, for example. You can still be as idealistic as you've always been or you can choose to be part of the new commercial breed. You don't lose anything by having somebody else come in and give you a new option. Before, obviously you couldn't choose anything but being pure.

By the way, I've never felt that I was in the idealistic camp. Sure I've always seen open source as a way of making the world a better place. But more than that, I see it as a way of having fun. That's not very idealistic.

And I have always thought that idealistic people are interesting, but kind of boring and sometimes scary.

In order to hold a very strong opinion, you have to exclude all the other opinions. And that means you have to become unreasonable. This is one of the problems I have with American politics vis-à-vis European politics. In the American version of the game, you draw the enemy lines and the skill rests on one side's ability to be divisive. European politicians tend to win by demonstrating they can foster cooperation.

So I'm stuck with the conciliatory approach. The only time I was ever nervous about commercialism was very early on, when Linux didn't have much of a name. At that point, if commercial people had coopted Linux, there would have been nothing I could do. But that's obviously not the case now. One concern raised in newsgroup flames amid the activity of 1998 was that commercial people wouldn't give anything back. To some extent, I had to trust the new corporate players as much as Linux developers were trusting me. And they proved themselves to be trustworthy. They haven't held back. So far it's been very positive.

As poster boy, holder of the Linux trademark, maintainer of the Linux kernel, I felt a growing sense of responsibility. I felt increasingly responsible for the fact that millions of people now relied on Linux, and immense pressure to make sure it worked as reliably as possible. It was important to me to help corporations understand what open source was all about. There was no war, as far as I was concerned, between the greedy corporations and the altruistic hackers.

No, I wasn't giving up my ideals by meeting with Intel when they asked me to help them deal with the Pentium FO OF lockup bug ("Pentium FO OF bug?" I hear you ask. Yeah, it's us whacky engineers, making up whacky names again. "FO OF" is the hexadecimal representation of the first two bytes of an illegal instruction sequence that made Pentium CPUs lock up. Thus the name). No, it wasn't hypocritical to promote the wonders of open source code while collecting a salary from a company that was so closed it wouldn't even tell people what it was doing. The fact is, I respected, and still do, the low-power chip Transmeta was developing, and I saw it as the most interesting technology project out there—and the one with the broadest possible implications. And, for the record, I was part of an effort to get the company to release at least some of its code.

I felt pressure to hold my ground within the open source community as someone who could be trusted from both a technology standpoint and an ethical standpoint. It was important to me not to take sides among competing Linux companies. No, I wasn't selling out by accepting stock options that Red Hat was kind enough to offer me as thanks. But it did make sense to turn down the entrepreneur in London who was offering me $10 million just to lend my name to his fledgling Linux company as a board member. He couldn't fathom that I would turn down such a huge amount for such little heavy lifting. It was like, *"What part of ten million dollars don't you understand?"*

It hadn't occurred to me that I might face such issues. And Linux's newfound popularity brought with it some tricky times not just for me but for the entire virtual community. In fact, as open source code gained the world's attention in 1998, one of the big debates dealt with the name itself. Until then we had referred to the phenomenon of sharing software, under such licenses as the GP, as "free software," and in general referred to the "free software movement." The term has its roots in the Free Software Foundation, which was founded by Richard Stallman in 1985 to promote free software projects such as GNU, the free Unix he launched. Suddenly, evangelizers like Eric Raymond were finding that journalists were confused. Did the word "free" mean it didn't cost anything? Did it mean "free" as in no restrictions? Did it mean "free" as in freedom? It turned out that Brian Behlendorf, who was talking to journalists on behalf of Apache, was encountering similar frustrations. After weeks of private email exchanges in which I was not a participant but was merely cc:ed (I wasn't interested in the political side), a consensus was reached: We would refer to it as "open" instead of "free." Hence, the free software movement became the open source movement—for people who preferred to see it as a movement, which I guess it was. However, the Free Software Foundation is still called the Free Software Foundation, and Richard Stallman is still the psychological mastermind behind it.

As one of the de facto leaders of that movement, I was increasingly in demand. Every time my phone rang at Transmeta—and it rang all the time those days—it meant one of two things: Either a journalist wanted to interview me, or the organizers of a conference wanted me to speak. In order to spread the word about open source and Linux, I felt obligated to do both. Take a shy math wiz, put him on the greet-and-grin circuit for a populist cause, and you've created a folk hero. Forget what Eric Raymond said about me being less visibly odd than a lot of hackers. A big part of my appeal (or whatever you want to call it) is that I *wasn't* Bill Gates.

Journalists seemed to love the fact that, while Gates lived in a high-tech lakeside mansion, I was tripping over my daughters' playthings in our new location—a three-bedroom ranch house of a duplex with bad plumbing in boring Santa Clara. And that I drove a boring Pontiac. And answered my own phone. Who *wouldn't* love me?

As Linux came to be viewed as a real threat to Microsoft— and at the time of Microsoft's antitrust woes, it sure needed at least the appearance of a real threat—the press jumped on every development as if it were covering World War III. Somebody leaked the "Halloween Document," an internal Microsoft memo indicating that the company was concerned about Linux. Soon Steve Balmer was quoted as saying, "Sure, I'm worried." The fact was, even if Microsoft stood to benefit by playing up the competition its Windows NT was getting from Linux, the reality was that the competition would only get more intense.

I didn't *have to* stand on a soap box and say horrible things about Microsoft. What would be the point? Events just play themselves out, and they played themselves out in favor of Linux. Journalists loved it all. The Softspoken (like a fox) David vs. the Monopolistic, Meanspirited Goliath. And, since I'm being completely candid, I actually enjoyed talking about it all to reporters. I like to call journalists scum, but I found most of my interviews to be fun. The reporters typically were interested in our story—who wouldn't root for the underdog?

Once they got their fill of the Amoeba-that-Destroyed-Microsoft plot (note: in the interest of full disclosure, this sentence has been spell-checked by a Microsoft product), journalists wanted to understand the concept of open source. That message was taking less and less time to get across, since people could now see examples of it in action. What seemed to amaze them next was the administration of Linux. They couldn't grasp how the largest collaborative project in the history of humanity could possibly be managed so effectively when the average thirty-person company typically degenerates into something resembling barnyard chaos.

Somebody coined the phrase "Benevolent Dictator" to describe how I ran the whole thing. The first time I heard the term, all I could think of was some sunny-nation general with a dark mustache handing out bananas to his starving masses. I don't know if I feel comfortable with the Benevolent Dictator image. I control the Linux kernel, the foundation of it all, because, so far, everybody connected with Linux trusts me more than they trust anyone else. My method for managing the project with hundreds of thousands of developers is the same as it was when I coded away in my bedroom: I don't proactively delegate as much as I wait for people to come forward and volunteer to take over things. It started when I divested myself of the responsibilities I found less interesting, like the user-level code. People stepped forward and offered to take over the subsystems. Everything filters up to me through the maintainers of those subsystems.

I approve or disapprove of their work, but mostly I let things happen naturally. If two people are maintaining similar kinds of things, I accept both of them to see which gets used. Sometimes they both get used but wind up taking different paths. Once, there was intense competition between two people who insisted on sending patches that fought each other's patches. I refused to accept patches from either, until one of the developers lost interest. That's how King Solomon would have handled things if he ran a preschool.

Benevolent dictator? No, I'm just lazy. I try to manage by not making decisions and letting things occur naturally. That's when you get the best results.

My approach made headlines.

But the irony here is that while my Linux management style, such as it is, was earning high marks in the press, I was an undeniable failure during my brief stint as a manager at Transmeta. At one point, it was decided that I should manage a team of developers. I flopped. As anyone who has ventured into my junk heap of an office knows, I'm totally disorganized. I had trouble managing the weekly progress meetings, the performance reviews, the action items. After three months it became obvious that my management style wasn't doing anything to help Transmeta, despite the praise I was getting from journalists for the way I was running Linux.

Meanwhile, the press kept pounding away at another issue: fragmentation. Those who have followed the rocky, unhappy history of Unix know about the endless bickering between Unix vendors. The question came up all the time in 1998: Would history repeat itself in the world of Linux? My answer was always that while there undoubtedly is bickering among Linux vendors, it can't lead to the fragmentation that has kept Unix a perennial almost-been. The problem with Unix is that competing vendors wasted years implementing similar features, simply because they didn't have access to the same source base. Developing the same features independently not only cost Unix years but it also led to bloody infighting. Sure, I would tell the press, Linux vendors don't host regularly scheduled Love-Ins. But there is and will continue to be less fragmentation inside the Linux community than in the Unix community, because even Linux vendors who are not friendly can see the same source base and can reuse each other's work. The source code is a repository from which anyone can draw.

The more journalists started grasping such concepts, the more I liked meeting them. (Unlike the journalists I remember from my youth in Helsinki, most of them in the United States in the 1990s were sober.) I particularly enjoyed the opportunity to debate with them.

But speaking was another matter entirely. I'm not what you'd call a natural performer. Remember: I'm the fellow who barely left his bedroom throughout his childhood. I never was very good at even *writing* speeches, so I always waited until the night before an event to prepare.

Somehow, that didn't seem to matter. Typically, I would step out to the podium and people would rise to their feet and applaud even before I opened my mouth. I don't want to sound unappreciative, but I've always found that to be an embarrassing situation. Anything you say sounds wrong, even my standard, "Thanks, Now Please Sit Down." I'm open to suggestions.

But not all the calls were from journalists or conference organizers. One night I was sitting at home with Tove. We were reading to the girls. The phone rang.

I answered: "Torvalds."

"Uh. Is this the Linux guy?"

"Yes."

Two seconds of silence. *Click.*

Another night a fellow from Las Vegas phoned me at home, trying to get me to sign on with some Linux T-shirt business.

The obvious solution would have been to get an unlisted phone number. I didn't bother to do that when we first moved to California because it was more expensive than having a listed number. I've since learned the price you pay for being so frugal, and am now unlisted. Once, before I got de-listed, David misplaced my home number and phoned directory assistance. He asked for my number, and the operator who provided it said with great astonishment, *"He's listed? With all his millions?"*

But no, there weren't millions. Millions of Linux users, sure. Not millions of dollars for Linus.

And that was perfectly fine.

VII.

Most days I wake up thinking I'm the luckiest bastard alive. I don't remember if Wednesday, August 11, 1999 was one of those days, but it should have been.

It was the second day of the Linux World convention and trade show which had been taking place at the San Jose Convention Center. Dirk Hohndel, who is CEO of SuSE and traveled from Germany for the trade show, had spent the night on the guest bed in our family room. I've known him for years. He's one of the old XFree86 people, and is on the graphics side of Linux. He's also Daniela's godfather. I woke up, made cappuccino for Tove and Dirk, read everything in the San Jose Mercury News except the sports pages and the classified ads—like I always do—and then we piled into the Toyota Rav4 for the ten-mile trip to downtown San Jose.

I remember shaking a lot of hands.

This was the day that Red Hat would be going public. The company had years earlier given me stock options, and had only recently sent me some paperwork that I never bothered to look at. It sat somewhere in a stack of papers near my computer. I remember I really wanted Red Hat to do well. It wasn't so much a matter of being excited about the options—I didn't quite realize what they meant. I was extremely jazzed for another reason. In many respects, the IPO's success would be a validation of Linux. So I was a bit nervous that morning, but I wasn't the only one. The market had been doing poorly for weeks, and people wondered whether or not Red Hat would even pull off its IPO.

The "liquidity event" did, in fact, happen. We got word on the conference floor that Red Hat's initial public offering came in at $15. Or was it $18? I don't remember. The important thing was that it ended the first day of trading at $35. Nothing record-breaking, but it was okay.

I remember driving home with Tove and Dirk in the car, first feeling relieved. Then, when I thought about the money, growing excited. Only when we were stuck in Northbound traffic on Highway 101 did it strike me that in one day I had gone from basically zero to half a million dollars. My heart started beating faster. It was elation tempered with disbelief.

I was clueless about stock and decided I needed to find out what to do next. So I phoned Larry Augustin, VA Linux's CEO. I told him he was the only person I knew who had a clue about how stock works. My exact words: "Do you have like a stockbroker or somebody that you trust because I don't want to go on eBay?"

Red Hat had given me options—not an outright grant of stock. I didn't know what to do about exercising them. I knew there might be a lockup period but I didn't know if it applied to me, and I hadn't thought about the tax consequences. Larry, who is good at this sort of thing and who knows a lot of people, got me in touch with this guy at Lehman Brothers, who shouldn't have been handling me at all because I wasn't a big customer. He promised to find out what I should do. Meanwhile, two days after the IPO, I got an email from someone in Red Hat's Human Resources Department, or their lawyer, in which they mentioned something about the stock having split before the IPO. I knew nothing about it. So I tracked down the manila envelope containing all the stock option paperwork I had never bothered to read, and there it was, in plain (for legalese) English: My options had magically doubled.

My half-million dollars was actually a *million* dollars!

Regardless of the image that has caught on in the press, of me as a selfless geek-for-the-masses living under a vow of poverty, I was, frankly, delirious.

There, I said it.

I sat down and read all the Red Hat papers. Yes, I was subject to a 180-day lockup.

Do you have any idea how long 180 days can be when you're a first-time millionaire on paper?

Now I had a new sport (or a sport, period): keeping track of Red Hat's stock price, which continued escalating during the following six months. It went up gradually and jumped a few times and just grew and grew. At one point, Red Hat even split once more. At best, I was worth $5 million from the options.

Red Hat started relatively low and inched skyward as Wall Street, in the throes of its love affair with anything even remotely related to the Internet, "discovered" Linux. We were the Flavor of the Month during the cold-weather months at the end of 1999. Investment pundits on television and in the general press couldn't get enough of this crazy little operating system that was promising to upend Microsoft. My phone rang constantly. It all reached a stunning climax with the VA Linux IPO on December 9th. That was an endorsement beyond anyone's expectation.

Larry Augustin and I went up to San Francisco to be on site at the offices of First Boston Credit Suisse for the IPO. I was wearing what I always wear: a freebie T-shirt and sandals. We brought our wives and kids. It was a crazy scene with the toddlers running around among the buttoned-down investment bankers.

It all happened so suddenly. Figures streamed across monitors indicating that VA Linux, on the first day of trading, was selling in the $300-a-share range. This was unheard of. Even if we hadn't seen the figures, we would have known it was a record because of the way the investment bankers were hypnotized by CNN and the Bloomberg financial channel. For his part, Larry was his usual cool self. I don't think he batted an eyelash during the whole thing. I wouldn't know for sure, because I was busy chasing after my daughters.

Even the dwellers of Madagascar's rainforests probably were aware of how rich it all made Larry. He had driven up to San Francisco without much of a financial net worth, and drove back to Silicon Valley worth something on the order of $1.6 billion. And, as the press continually pointed out, he was still in his twenties.

For my part, I had been given a stock grant and options for shares in VA Linux. As with Red Hat, I couldn't sell shares for six months. But unlike Red Hat, which climbed steadily, VA Linux had nowhere to go but down. After its record-setting opening day, the stock dropped steadily for a year, reaching a low point of 6.62. Partly, the stock was a victim of the market correction that hurt most technology stocks that April. But also, Linux's stint as Flavor of the Month had ended with the spring thaw. Because of the VA Linux lockup period, I couldn't take advantage of the hyper market while it lasted. It was psychologically much harder to follow the company than it had been to follow Red Hat, to know that every night when I crawled into bed, I would wake up with a lessened financial net worth.

But I still felt like the luckiest bastard alive.

Linus drives up to my Sausalito office one evening in January. After snickering about my use of a Macintosh and a non-Linux operating system, he sits down to read the first draft of a lengthy preface I have written, which is in the first person, from his perspective. I sit maybe two inches away. The only noise Linus makes is when he trips over a line about how he never expected to find himself the only global superstar Finland has produced other than Jean Sibelius and Nikki the Reindeer. After maybe ten minutes, he finishes the preface and his only comment is: "Boy, you write long sentences." We spend a couple of hours making the sentences shorter and changing some of the language to words that he would actually use, and learning how to collaborate at work, having already proven that we are champs at goofing off collaboratively. We eventually ditched that preface.

Then Linus attempts, unsuccessfully, to improve the resolution on my flat screen. It was last year's state-of-the-art computer screen, and I thought of it as something of a status symbol. "How can you read from this thing?" he asks. He is unsuccessful at improving the resolution quality to meet his standards. Then he takes out a piece of paper and starts drawing diagrams and explaining how monitors work. At some point I say, "Hey, let's grab some sushi."

"This money thing is driving me crazy," he says. "Just the waiting for the lock-up period to end. It's like having lots of money but not having lots of money. It's on my mind constantly."

I order saki. He orders fruit juice because he is driving.

"Up until now, we almost never had more than $5,000 in our

checking account. Except for some stocks and stuff we have for savings that we can't touch, that was all the money we had to spend. So now I have all this money on paper and—"

"Like how much money? A couple of million?"

"How about $20 million? That's what the stock from the VA Linux IPO is worth, as long as it doesn't drop. But I don't have access to the money until the lock-up period in six months. No, now it's five months."

"I don't see the problem here. You have to wait five months before buying a big house? I don't mean to be unsympathetic but . . ."

"Hey, well it seems at first that it's enough money that we should be able to buy any house we want. But we need a house with five bedrooms and we want enough land around the house so we can hear animals and I've been playing pool everyday at work so we'll need a room that's big enough to hold a pool table. And we want a separate unit for when Tove's parents visit, or so we can have my sister's friends come from Finland and stay a few months and help us with the kids. It's funny, we had Patricia when we moved from Finland to the states. We had Daniela when we moved from our apartment to the duplex, and . . ."

"So you guys are working on having another kid?"

"Well, we're letting things happen naturally."

"Where I come from, you pronounce that, 'We're trying to have another kid,' dude."

"Okay. So we'll need more space and we've gone to a couple of Open Houses and the houses available are unbelievably expensive. I mean you get $20 million and it's like, wow, I can afford any house in the world. But we looked at a house for $1.2 million in Woodside that had no land and was really trashy. The best house we saw was for $5 million. But if you have $20 million, you've gotta figure that half of that goes to taxes. Then you have $10 million to work with, but the taxes on a house like that could be like $60,000 a year, so you've got to set money aside for that. And I don't know. This is going to be the only time in my life when I'll get so much money and I don't want to overextend myself and not be able to afford to live in the house. And we don't want to have a mortgage hanging over our heads."

"I'm not feeling sorry for you. First of all, you'll probably do okay if Transmeta does okay in an IPO."

"Yeah. But I'm only a junior engineer, so I'm not getting that much stock. And my salary isn't that high."

"Linus, you could go to any venture capitalist in this town and get anything you wanted . . ."

"I guess you're right."

VIII.

This is the place where I slip in my golden rules. Number One is: "Do unto others as you would want them to do unto you." If you follow that rule, you'll always know how to behave in any situation. Number Two is: "Be proud of what you do." Number Three: "And have fun doing it."

Of course, it's not always easy to be proud and have fun. A month before the VA Linux IPO, I accomplished neither when I delivered a keynote speech at the 1999 Comdex Show in Las Vegas. Comdex, as most everyone knows, is the biggest, baddest trade show known to humanity. For most of a week, the sleepy town of Las Vegas, Nevada, becomes a magnet for every conceivable high-tech product that could possibly be peddled and the masses of people who would buy and sell them. It's the only time of the year when you can roll down the window of a Las Vegas cab, lean out, and ask a random hooker strutting past: "What time is the keynote?"—and she'll know the answer.

It was a big deal that the trade show organizers asked the benevolent dictator of Planet Linux to give a Comdex keynote speech. It was the computer industry's way of acknowledging that Linux was a force with which to be reckoned.

Bill Gates delivered the keynote on Sunday, the first night of the show. He had attracted a standing-room crowd in the Venetian Hotel ballroom, which is about the size of seven average IKEA stores. Conference-goers who were eager to hear what he had to say about the antitrust trial—which was happening at the time—or who just wanted to be able to tell their grandchildren they had seen the world's richest man in the flesh, lined up hours beforehand in a snake pattern in the Hotel conference center's massive basement level. Gates's speech began with a lawyer joke, then included well-choreographed demonstrations of Microsoft Web technology and highly polished video segments, one of them with Gates dressed like and imitating Austin Powers—that sent the audience into fits of laughter.

I wasn't there. I was helping Tove shop for a bathing suit.

But the following night, I delivered my speech in the same room.

I would have rather gone shopping. Well, not really . . .

It's not that I wasn't prepared. Ordinarily I write my speech the day before, but this time I actually got a head start. It was a Monday night speech and on Saturday I had written it and set up the computer to project its slides. Everything looked really good. I had even put my speech on three different floppies, just to protect myself in case one of them might turn out bad. The one thing I hate more than speaking is speaking when something goes wrong. I even put my speech on the Internet, just in case *all* the floppies were bad.

There was a Comdex-inspired traffic jam on the Strip so we arrived at the Venetian Hotel only a half-hour before I was due to begin. I was with Tove and the girls and some folks from the show. When we finally got into the building, we had problems getting access to the backstage area because one of the organizers had misplaced the security badges. I mean, everything went wrong.

So finally we got inside. I would have been nervous if I were about to speak before forty people, let alone the biggest audience of my life. Then it happened.

I discovered that the computer itself, which had been so painstakingly set up two days earlier, was nowhere to be found. It was insane. Someone mentioned that people had started lining up for the speech downstairs more than four hours in advance, and that the waiting area was packed to capacity. Meanwhile, we were running around like hens without heads, searching backstage for the machine.

It was a normal desktop system with Star Office, one of the Linux office suites, installed. And I was supposed to just put in my floppy and go. Everything had been set up so that there wouldn't even be any cables to attach. *But the computer had vanished.* Apparently the machine had somehow gotten mislabeled or something, so it was shipped back. Happily, I had my laptop with me and I had the actual slide file of my speech on the laptop and I did have Star Office installed.

Because this was my laptop, I didn't have all the right fonts. That meant that the last line on all my slides was missing. When I realized this, I thought: *Who cares? I'm going to get through this alive.* Then we had to hook up all the cables. I mean, literally, they started letting people in before everything was set up. I was up there, still trying to get it to work, as a flood of humanity washed into the humongous auditorium, filling every available seat and then filling the standing area along the sides. Luckily, they gave me the standing ovation *before* I opened my mouth.

I started out with some lame reference to the lawyer joke that Bill Gates used to open his speech. I gave a one-sentence hint about what then-secretive Transmeta was developing. It had been wildly rumored in the press that I would use the Comdex speech as an occasion to (finally) announce Transmeta's chip. But we were just not ready. The main part of my speech simply involved ticking off the benefits of open source computing. I wasn't in a mood to crack as many jokes as I ordinarily do. At one point, Daniela—who was sitting with Tove and Patricia in the first row—began a crying spell that was probably audible throughout Las Vegas's casinos and strip clubs.

That was not a speech that will go down in history among

the great orations. Later, someone tried to cheer me up by inform-ing me that Bill Gates, too, had been visibly nervous on the same stage the night before. However, his onstage apparatus had worked without a hitch. The trouble was, he had the U.S. Depart-ment of Justice breathing down his neck. I guess I came out ahead.

It seemed like a strategy out of Journalism 101: Find the person who had been waiting the longest to hear Linus's keynote, and hang out with him (undoubtedly, him) in line. What better way to gather insight into the dweebie hordes who follow Linus like he's some sort of vendorware-clad God.

At 5 P.M. I'm on an escalator descending into Geek Woodstock. At the head of the vast, snaking line is an intense computer science student from Walla Walla College who eagerly agrees to let me join him. He has been waiting, so far, two and a half hours to see Linus, and he will be waiting another two and a half hours before being let into the auditorium. His classmates, who are behind him in line, arrived in the queue maybe half an hour after he did. They drove down from Washington State with one of their professors and are sleeping in the gymnasium of a local high school. They all seem to have started their own Web design business. They seem to have conveniently divided up the universe of grownups into two groups—hackers and suits—and are constantly pointing out members of the latter category in the growing line, saying things like, "Man, look at all the suits here," the way their Delta Tau Chi counterparts might survey a beach during spring break and observe, "Man, look at all the foxes here." But like their Delta Tau Chi counterparts, they are doing all the usual horseplay—slapping each other high-fives, trading insults, although the insults all relate to motherboards or gigabytes.

And then they talk about Linus. His name comes across capitalized, as in "LINUS wouldn't work at a company that wasn't going to be open source, He just wouldn't." They have been slavish scrutinizers of slashdot and other Web sites where rumors of Transmeta's hushed goings-on circulate like the lurid details of a Hollywood starlet's love life. This mania and the speculation/fascination isn't happening only among the ardent groupies who arrived here first.

I visit the men's room and take my place at the only empty urinal, interrupting a conversation in progress.

"This speech is going to be way boring compared to the Gates keynote," says the fellow to my left.

"What do you expect?" replies the other guy. "Linus is a hacker, not a suit. I mean, give him a break."

When we finally get into the auditorium, somehow we are not up front but toward the back of the middle. My line-mate from Walla Walla forgets, for a moment, about the excitement of seeing his hero live, and goes into a rage about not being in the first row, where he deserves to be. Soon, he is pointing out the suits in the audience. Even though we're maybe seventy-five yards from the front, it's possible to catch a glimpse of Linus on the darkened stage, seated at a computer. He quickly types into the computer while being surrounded by a few officials. What could be happening up there? Some sort of last-minute software demonstration?

Eventually, Linus and the others leave the stage. Somehow Linus International Executive Director Maddog (Jon Hall) is introduced. My companion from Walla Walla gets visibly excited. "Check out the beard," he says. Then, Maddog announces how pleased he is to introduce a man who is like a son to him. Linus reemerges and gets a big hairy hug from Maddog. Even from back in the cheap seats, I could tell he was nervous.

"I wanted to start with a lawyer joke, but that was taken," he says, a reference to antitrust-suit-plagued Bill Gates's well-received opening the previous night: "Anybody heard any good lawyer jokes?"

He proceeds to give a one-sentence hint at Transmeta's secretive operation. Then the rest of his speech consists of rattling off the sentences that are flashed on slides high above his head, statements about the growing importance of open source. Nothing surprising. Nothing new.

It is delivered in a tired-but-cheerful monotone. At one point, one of his daughters cries.

In mid-sentence he says, "That's my kid." You could look up at the monitor and see the stage lighting reflecting off the beads of sweat on his forehead.

Afterward, audience members line up for questions. He quickly declines to say which of the Linux word processing software he prefers. When someone asks him how many stuffed penguins he has at home, he answers: "Quite a few." An audience member asks how he likes living in California, to which he responds by rhapsodizing about the weather. "It's November and I'm still wearing shorts. In Helsinki I'd have lost my crown jewels by now." A fan walks up to the microphone for audience questions and announces, simply, "Linus, you're my hero." To which Linus responds, as if he has heard the same statement a million times and answered it a million times: "Thanks."

After the questions are over, hundreds of people flood into the area below the podium, where Linus has now moved and is shaking as many hands as he possibly can.

IX.

Is the Linux Revolution Over?

By Scott Berinato, PC Week

"Thank you for calling. The Revolution is over. If you would like further information on Linux, please press one . . ."

It appears Linus Torvalds has a handler, which must mean this whole Linux thing is mainstream, so forget about the revolution and get back to work on your Windows desktops.

Once was a time when reporters could call the inventor of the Linux operating system at his office at cloak-and-dagger marketed Transmeta Corp., punch in his extension and receive a familiar declarative "Torvalds" from the man himself on the other end. He was patient and he answered your questions. He told you when he had no time. Sometimes he told you when you asked useless neophyte programmer questions. But he answered the phone.

Today, when you call Transmeta and punch in his extension, a pleasant female voice greets you. "Thank you for calling Linus Torvalds. This voice mail does not accept messages. To contact him, please send a fax to . . ."

What? And it starts to sink in: He's not getting back to you. He's had enough. He's a celebrity and getting a quick interview with him now will be like getting a quick interview with that other *big computer industry celebrity. The woman rattles off a fax num-*

ber and you're already thinking of hitting the old 0-# combo for a receptionist . . .

"Our receptionists do not take messages for him, nor do they keep his calender." D'oh. She's pleasant. The worst. "But they will gladly get your fax to him." Uh-huh. And Bill will gladly break up Microsoft to appease David Boies.

Okay, so the Linux revolution isn't over, but like any revolution, the rag-tag riff-raff is being superseded by mainstream sympathizers. Suburban new wave supplanted urban punk rock. Wealthy landowners in the colonies rose up after the poor taxed man. (The wealthy landowners, by the way, later tried to foist on frontiersmen a whiskey tax not so different from the tea tax imposed on them a few years earlier.)

In fact, it's probably high time Linus stepped back. It was inevitable, really, given the number of press calls and the maddening range of topics he was fielding.

Take his press Q+A session at the Linux World Expo in San Jose earlier this month. Torvalds, who agreed to the session because he simply didn't have time to field the innumerable individual requests, first had to rattle off what were becoming familiar answers to familiar questions. Can open source work in the business world? Are you trying to rule software the way Bill Gates rules software? What do you think of Microsoft? What is open source? What is Linux? Why a penguin?

Torvalds, by this point, was clearly entering the canned realm of sports figures with his answers. Think Tim Robbins in Bull Durham: "I just need to go out there and give 110 percent to try and help the team . . ."

And beyond the redundant, the questions from journalists outside the tech world veered wildly. At one point during his press conference, the Finnish phenom was asked how he was going to capture *the small and medium business market. (Typically Torvaldian retort: "I personally haven't tried to capture anyone.") Two questions later, an eager, I've-got-a-unique-angle-to-this-open-source-mess reporter asked Torvalds what he thought of corporations patenting agricultural genomes. (Typically quotable Torvaldian response: "I'm of two minds when it comes to patents. There are good bad ones and really bad ones.")*

Programmers, heed this: If someone starts asking you about agricultural genomes, it's likely time to get a handler.

So maybe it's a good thing that Linus doesn't answer his phone anymore. Still, we'll miss the candor and self-deprecation of Torvalds, which came across so genuinely to reporters used to burning their throats on the dry, pressurized-airplane-air marketing being blown by most companies. And we hope, if faxes do in fact reach his desk, and he does in fact respond to questions, he will keep the Torvaldian tone.

Because if the faux-pleasant PR voices take over, this Linux thing won't be nearly so much fun.

Okay, I guess I owe Mr. Berinato an explanation, but not an apology.

Anyone reading this column would assume the mounting pressures of my role as chief nerd had turned me into an asshole. But that's wrong. I always was an asshole.

I'll start at the beginning. I think voice mail is evil. It is the perfect example of a bad technology. In fact it is the worst technology that exists, and I hate it with a passion. So at Transmeta we started out with a per-user voice mail system that allowed each employee to store twenty minutes worth of messages. After that, callers got the message saying the mailbox was full, please contact the receptionist. Mine was always full.

I think it was the journalists who caused the backlash. They would badger the Transmeta receptionists because my voice mailbox was full. After the first hundred times, the receptionists started getting irritated. They knew I wasn't interested and they didn't want to be the ones telling people to fuck off.

So I started deleting messages without listening to them, just so the front desk people wouldn't get annoyed. Most of the time I would never listen to my messages, anyway. For one thing, people usually mumble their phone numbers into the recording, and I would have to listen fifteen times just to figure out what they've said. Also, I refuse to call people back if I have no reason to call them back. People would get a warm and fuzzy feeling that they had left a message. Until they realized I wouldn't return their call.

That's when they would call the receptionist. The receptionist wouldn't know what to say, so I would tell him or her to tell the caller to fax me. Faxes are as easy to ignore as voice mail, although at least with a fax you could make out the number, should you want to. I never wanted to.

At first, the receptionist politely told callers to please send me a fax. Eventually, people caught on to the fact that I didn't read the fax, and they would call back a week later and complain that they had already faxed me. So the receptionist again got caught in the middle. It wasn't her job to handle my calls.

Yes, Mr. Berinato's generous description of me in the good old days before Linux took off notwithstanding, I truly always have been an asshole. This isn't anything new.

The fax solution didn't last that long. In the end, they set up a special phone-messaging account for me that didn't have voice mail. By this time Transmeta had hired a PR person who volunteered to handle my requests. They're trained to do this, I'm told. They still tell me I should always call journalists back because, even if I don't want to talk to them, reporters get a warm and fuzzy feeling that I returned their call. My reaction to that is: I don't care about their warm and fuzzies.

Okay. I do answer my own phone to callers who happen to

call while I'm sitting at my desk. But that shouldn't be interpreted as an attempt to appear accessible. And it certainly isn't a political statement. The point about open source has never been that I'm more accessible than anybody else. It's never been that I'm more accessible than anybody else. It's never been that I'm more open to other people's suggestions. That's never been the issue. The issue is that even if I'm the blackest demon from Hell, even if I'm outright evil, people can choose to ignore me because they can just do the stuff themselves. It's not about me being open, it's about them having the power to ignore me. That's important.

There's no "official" version of Linux. There's my version and there's everybody else's version. The fact is, most people trust my version and rely on it as the de facto official version because they've seen me work for nine years on it. I was the original guy and people generally agree that I've been doing a good job. But let's say I shave my head to display a 666 and say, "Bow before me because if you don't I will smite thee!" They would just laugh in my face and say, "OK, we'll just take this little kernel and do what we think is right."

People trust me. But the only reason they do is that so far I've been trustworthy.

That doesn't mean I'm willing to listen to voice mail—or to anyone who happens to reach me on the phone. I've never felt that people should see me as this good guy who likes to respond to anyone who calls or sends me email. And while we're on the subject, it's strange to have these stories making me out to be this self-effacing monk or saint who just doesn't care about money at all. I have tried over the years to dispel that myth, but my efforts never make it into print. I don't want to be the person the press wants me to be.

The fact is, I've always hated that self-effacing monk image because it's so uncool. It's a boring image. And it's untrue.

X.

Crawling out of my bedroom and into the spotlight, I quickly had to learn the sort of tricks of living that other people probably picked up en route to kindergarten. For example, I never could have anticipated how ridiculously seriously people would take me—or my every move. Here are two situations, both of them variations on a theme.

Back at the university, I had a root account on my machine. Every account has a name associated with it. The name is used for informational purposes. So I named the root account on my machine Linus "God" Torvalds. I was God of that machine, which sat in my office at the university. Is that such a big deal?

Now, when somebody "fingers" a machine under Linux, or Unix, they are checking to see who's logged on to that machine. Due to the advent of firewalls, the act of fingering doesn't take place much anymore. But years ago people would finger another's machine to see if the user had logged on or had read his email. It was also a way of checking out someone's "plan," personal information the person had posted on their machine, sort of a predecessor to web pages. My plan always included the latest kernel version. So one way for people to figure out the version of the day was to finger my machine. Some people had even automated the process. They would finger me once an hour as a way of keeping up on version changes. Regardless, whenever someone fingered me, they would see that my root account was named Linus God Torvalds. This wasn't a problem early on. Then I started getting emails from people who told me that was blasphemy. So I eventually changed it. These are people who take themselves too seriously, and that drives me crazy.

Then, of course, there was the incident in North Carolina. Guds! That was bad. A recently published book about Red Hat made it sound like an international incident of potentially catastrophic proportions. It wasn't really much.

I had been invited to speak at a meeting of Linux users hosted by Red Hat, which is based in Durham. The auditorium was packed. The moment I walked out onto the stage, everybody rose to their feet and started cheering. The first words out of my mouth were the first thing that came to mind:

"I am your God."

It was meant to be a joke, for crying out loud!

It wasn't, "I really am convinced that I am your God and you should never forget it." It was: "Okay, okay, okay. I know I'm your God. Now please just sit down and hold your appreciation until after you actually hear what I have to say, although I genuinely do appreciate your preemptive appreciation."

I can't believe I'm willingly reliving this.

After my four-word greeting, everyone was silent for a moment. Hours later, those four words had become the topic of newsgroup postings. I admit it: It was tasteless, but unintentionally tasteless. Actually, it was probably my way of dealing with the embarrassment of having people stand up and applaud you just because you step out to the speaker's podium.

People take me too seriously. They take a lot of things too seriously. And one lesson I've learned from my years as Linux's hood ornament is that there's something worse: Some folks can't be content to just take things too seriously on their own. They're not happy unless they convince others to go along with their obsession. This has become one of my major pet peeves in life.

Have you ever stopped to think why dogs love humans so much? No, it's not because their owners take them to the groomers every six weeks and occasionally pick up what they leave behind on the sidewalk. It's because dogs love getting told what to do. It gives them a reason to live. (This is particularly important since so many of them are out of work—spayed or neutered, which means they've been laid off from their job as reproducers of new generations of canines. Also, with a few exceptions, there isn't much call for their wired-in jobs, like sniffing out rodents.) As a human, you're the leader of the pack and you're telling the dogs how they should behave. Following your orders is their passion. And they like it.

Unfortunately, that's how humans are built, too. People want to have somebody tell them what to do. It's in our kernel. Any social animal has to be that way.

It doesn't mean you're subservient. It just means that you are likely to go along with others when they tell you what to do.

Then there are people with individual ideas, folks who have convictions in certain areas to the degree that they say, "No, I won't go along." And these people become leaders. It's easy to become a leader. (It has to be. *I* became one, right?) Then, other people who don't have convictions in those areas are more than happy to let these leaders make their decisions for them and tell them what to do.

It's absolutely the right of any human being to do what they're told by someone they choose as a leader. I'm not arguing against that, although I find that part depressing. However, what I find to be unacceptable is when people, either leaders or followers, then try to impose their own world views on others. That's not just depressing—it's scary. It's depressing that people will follow just about anyone, including me. And it's scary that people will then want to impose their followingness—if that's a word—on others, including me.

Forget the clean-cut robot/proselytizers who always seem to bang on your door whenever you're on the computer, concentrating on a tricky technical problem, or whenever the kids are finally napping and you're just starting to get amorous. A more relevant example is close at hand in the open source community: the zealots who believe that *every* innovation should be licensed under the GPL ("GPL'd" in hacker parlance.) Richard Stallman wants to make everything open source. To him, it's a political struggle, and he wants to use the GPL as a way to drive open source. He sees no other alternative. The truth is, I didn't open source Linux for such lofty reasons. I wanted feedback. And it's how things were done in the early days of computers, when most of the work was done at universities or defense establishments and they ended up being very open. You gave your source away to another university when people asked for it. What Richard did, after getting cut off from projects he loved, was to be the first person to consciously open source.

Yes, there are enormous benefits to be gained by opening up one's technology and making it available under the same terms as Linux and a host of other innovations. To get a glimpse of those benefits, all you have to do is just look at the comparatively low standards of quality of any closed software project. The GPL and open source model allows for the creation of the best technology. It's that simple. It also prevents the hoarding of technology and ensures that anyone with an interest in a project or technology won't be excluded from its development.

This is not a minor point. Stallman, who deserves a monument in his honor for giving birth to the GPL, was inspired to jump-start the free software phenomenon mainly because he was shut out of a succession of interesting development projects when they moved from the open, academic world of the Massachusetts Institute of Technology to the proprietary corporate environment. The most notable of these was the LISP machine. LISP started out as part of the artificial intelligence community. As with many things, somebody thought it was so good that they should form a startup to make it a commercial success and make money on it. This happens all the time at universities. But Richard wasn't part of the commercial crowd, so when LISP became a commercial project under a company named Symbolics in 1981, suddenly he was cut off. To add insult to injury, Symbolics hired away many of his cohorts from the AI lab.

The same thing happened to him a few other times. The way I understand it, his motivation for promoting open source was not so much anticommercial as it was antiexclusion. For him, open source is about not getting left out. It's about being able to continue working on a project regardless of who makes it commercial.

The GPL is wonderful in its gift of letting anyone play. Just think about what a major advance for humanity that is! But does that mean that every innovation should be GPL'd?

No way! This is the abortion issue of technology. It should be up to the individual innovator to decide for herself or himself whether to GPL the project or to use a more conventional approach to copyright. The thing that drives me crazy about Richard is that he sees everything in black and white. And that creates unnecessary political divisions. He never understands the viewpoint of anybody else. If he were into religion, you would call him a religious fanatic.

In fact, the most annoying thing—second only to religious enthusiasts knocking on my door saying what I should believe in—is people knocking on my door (or bombarding me with email) saying how I should license my software. This should not be a political issue. People should be able to make up their own minds. It's one thing to suggest to someone that they consider GPLing their software, and then leaving it at that. It's another thing to argue the point. It's really bad when people complain about the fact that I work for a commercial company that doesn't GPL everything it does. I tell them it's not their business.

The thing I find hugely irritating about Richard is not that he believes that Linux—because its kernel relied on applications from the gnu software project—should more rightly be called "gnu/Linux." It is not that he openly resents me for being a poster boy for open source even though he was sharing code while I was still sleeping in a laundry basket. No, the reason I find him so pesty is that he continually complains about other people not using the GPL.

I admire Richard from afar for a bunch of reasons. And I guess I tend to respect people, like Richard, who have very strong moral opinions. But why can't they keep these opinions to themselves? The thing I dislike the most is when people tell me what I should or should not do. I absolutely despise people who think they have any say over my personal decisions. (Except, perhaps, my wife.)

Over the course of the development of Linux, pundits such as Eric Raymond have suggested that the operating system's success and the longevity of open source development have partly hinged on my pragmatic approach and my ability to keep from taking sides in disputes. While Eric is arguably the best articulator of the open-source phenomenon (and while I strongly, strongly disagree with his pro-gun sentiments), I believe he's a bit off the mark on his perception of me. It's not that I keep from taking sides. It's just that I so strongly resent anyone who tries to impose his or her morals on others. You can replace the word "morals" with "religion," "computing preferences," whatever.

Just as imposing morals is wrong, the next step—*institutionalizing* morals—is doubly wrong. I'm a big believer in individual choice, which means that I think I should make my own decisions when it comes to moral issues.

I want to decide for myself. I'm very much against unnecessary rules imposed by society. I'm a big believer that you should be able to do whatever you want in the privacy of your own home as long as you don't hurt anybody else. Any law saying otherwise is a very, very broken law. And there are laws that say otherwise. I find some scary rules, especially some that are imposed on schools and children. Imagine even thinking of imposing rules about teaching evolution, and taking that into the wrong direction. That I find scary. This is social conscience rearing its ugly head in places it really has nothing at all to do with.

At the same time, my personal belief is that what is more

important than me and my individual moral decisions is, not even the human race, but *evolution*. To that extent, I want my individual choices to take social issues into account. But that's probably built in. I think it is built into human biology—evolution—that we do take social things into account. Otherwise we'd have been gone long ago.

The only other thing worth ranting about: people who are too preachy. There's just no reason for folks to evangelize, and to be so self-righteous about it.

And I'm sounding just like one of them.

But it's an easy trap when people start taking you far too seriously.

XI.

Americans make a big fuss over March 17th (St. Patrick's Day), May 5th (Cinco de Mayo), and October 12th (Columbus Day), but hardly any attention is paid to December 6th, which as any Finn can tell you is Finnish Independence Day.

Most folks in Finland celebrate Finnish Independence Day the way they celebrate everything else, by partying to excess. They party-to-excess—even by Finnish standards—the night before and recover in front of the television set for almost the entire national holiday. The option, I guess, is to go out and trudge in the snow hung over.

What keeps everyone glued to their TV sets is a single event: the President's Ball. Finland doesn't have much in the way of high society so the President's Ball is pretty much it, the only truly big society event. It's televised nationally to keep people from driving with hangovers and to prove to ourselves that we can stage our own respectable version of the Academy Awards. No, a better metaphor: It's the Super Bowl of Finnish high society.

So throughout the day, from Utsjoki in the north to Hanko in the south, Finns munch on gravlax and aspirin as they watch a procession of invitees—men in tailcoats and women in outrageous (for Scandinavia) evening attire—shake hands with the president.

Nineteen hundred and ninety-nine was the year I got invited.

You automatically get invited if you're an ambassador to Finland or if you're part of the Finnish parliament. Maybe one hundred or two hundred random people are invited on various grounds. They may have won a medal in the Olympics or maybe they helped the president on his campaign. If you are the captain of the ice hockey team and you've just won the world championship, you get invited. If the operating system you created gains world-wide attention, you get an invitation. Spouses and companions come, too.

In fact, it was lucky that Tove and I could go at all. In August we had applied to the INS for permission to go to Finland and return. We weren't approved until early November. Two weeks later we received our invitation to the President's Ball.

Now imagine what it's like. Picture 2,000 Finns—and not even the most important 2,000 Finns—packed into the president's castle. It was a home that had been built for a Russian merchant. It really is just a large home, not exactly a one-family home but maybe a home for one family that has a lot of support—cooks, maids, and the like. It's not a huge place.

So you arrive. Someone takes your coat and then you're just jammed in there. You don't know where to go. Bowls of punch pro-liferate. Obviously, they contain vodka. This wouldn't be Finland if they didn't. It basically takes awhile to find people to talk to. You end up speaking to journalists, because, frankly, they're the most interesting people there. (Maybe it was the punch that made them seem more interesting than a parliament member from, say, Lahti.)

I didn't expect it to be much fun, because I wouldn't know many people there. I was the only one from the open source crowd invited. I expected it to be like the army—more enjoyable to talk about later. But it actually *was* fun.

Tove wore a green gown that would have been stunning and attracted media attention even if we were at the Oscars, not the Finnish President's Ball. Because she looked so good, and because Finland hadn't won the world ice hockey championship that year, the press dubbed us King and Queen of the Ball.

Whatever.

"You enter this house not as a journalist but as a friend. We are allowing no journalists in this house."

I had never seen Tove so ebullient. She greeted me at the door of the new house on the day she and Linus received the key. It's one of those monster homes: the Media Room (which now houses Linus's pool table) probably doesn't share a zip code with the Super Bonus Room, where Patricia and Daniela sleep, although it could handle an entire preschool. From the front door there's a wide, long angled hallway leading way back to the family room. If they remove the fancy Italian tiles, it will be a great place for the girls to practice skateboarding some day. Linus's office on the first floor has a mirrored sliding-glass door. Five bathrooms. Maybe they've found more of them by now. It's all in a gated community far from the heart of Silicon Valley.

Nicke Torvalds is visiting. Father and son return from a trip to the old duplex in a rented BMW Z3. It's the model Linus will soon be purchasing, and Nicke will drive it to the Stanford University library this afternoon. But first, he leans against the hot tub, situated in the unland-scaped backyard, and announces that this is the largest house anyone named Torvalds has ever owned. Then he takes a piece of paper and lists all twenty Torvaldses. He didn't know that a twenty-first was on its way.

Linus, too, is thrilled in the empty house. Nicke videotapes the surroundings and I ask Linus to carry Tove across the threshold so I can photograph the event. There's some very un-Finnish public displaying of affection.

"Did you ever think our house would be this big?" Tove asks me.

* * *

Tove needed to be on hand at the opening of the Ikea store in Emeryville to buy armoires for the new house, so I suggested Linus bring the kids over to a house I was renting in Stinson Beach. As soon as they arrived, I urged Linus to try out the kayak in the lagoon. He paddled around by himself, then with each of the girls, and climbed back onto the dock with wet pants.

I wanted Linus to give me his thoughts on a chapter entitled, "Will Success Spoil Me?" and took the girls outside to the beach so he could read it undisturbed. Patricia and Daniela spent maybe a half hour hunting for starfish and tiptoeing into the water, after which one of them announced "Kisin kommer," which translates to: "I've got to potty."

We returned to the house to find Linus sitting at the computer, in his underwear, a bag of pretzels at his side, intently typing away. It took him maybe fifteen seconds to realize we had arrived. He looked up from the monitor. His first words were: "Boy, your Macintosh sucks."

Then: "Oh, and I put my pants in your dryer."

He had retitled the chapter "Fame and Fortune," figuring that "Will Success Spoil Me?" sounded a bit egotistical. He wanted more time to write, so I took the girls out to search for seals while he finished the chapter.

XII.

It's easy to fight windmills if you don't realize how hard it is.

Five years ago when people asked me if I thought Linux would be able to take over the desktop and make a dent in Microsoft, they always had a doubtful edge to their voice. I invariably told them that I thought it would. They would look skeptical. The fact is, they probably knew more than I did about the reality.

I didn't really understand all the steps it would take to get there. Not only what it takes to tackle the technical problems of developing a robust and portable operating system, but what it takes to make that operating system a commercial, as well as technical, success. I would have been discouraged if I had known in advance just how much infrastructure would need to be in place to make Linux as successful as it has been. It's not only that you have to be good. You have to be good, sure, but everything has to turn out the right way, too.

Any sane person would have gazed up at the rugged mountainface that needed to be scaled, and would have been absolutely daunted. Just think about the technical problems of supporting PCs, which are about the most varied hardware out there. You have to support people who have bugs that you can't reproduce on applications that you don't even care about. But you care about Linux, so you care about helping to fix them.

Even to think about penetrating the commercial market, you have to have a respectable level of user support. From early on with Linux, you could have real support by doing it internally within a company. But to make it in a big way, you have to have a lot of people and a lot of infrastructure. It's not enough to have a 1-900 number or a 1-800 number for the first thirty days. To some extent, support is no longer much of an issue because it can be bought at any number of places—Linuxcare, Red Hat, IBM, Silicon Graphics, Compaq, Dell. But it clearly was something that had to be in place. For the longest time, I didn't even realize that. It has been a major challenge for years.

Unlike business people with solid technical backgrounds or journalists with a commercial bent, I was a narrowly focused software developer who was naive about what would be required. The technical problems alone would have kept me from embarking on this journey. If I had known how much work it would take, and that I would still be doing it ten years later—and that it would be almost a full-time job those entire ten years—I never would have started.

And the abuse! I don't get that much abuse these days, but it still happens. People who don't like open source or people who are just upset about bugs will send me email, cursing me over their frustrations. Compared to the amount of positive mail I get, it's minuscule. But it still happens.

Yes, if I had realized how much work and how hard, how difficult a lot of things would have been, I probably would not have done it. If I had had enough knowledge to understand the problems in advance, I probably never would have taken Linux far beyond its initial release. If I had known how much detail you have to get right, and how much people expect of an operating system, I would have been able to envision horror scenarios of things I couldn't handle.

But I also wasn't able to predict the upside. Like how much support I would get, and how many people would be working together on this. So now I change my mind. I guess if I had actually known the upside, I probably *would* have done it.

Intellectual Property

The intellectual property debate is so hot these days that I can't wander into a restroom without running across graffiti supporting one side or the other. Some people think that patents and other forms of intellectual property law are the bane of the free universe, and that these laws are not just misguided but actually *evil* and should be struck down as soon as possible. Others are convinced that pretty much the whole world economy is driven by intellectual property. And *those* people want to do anything to strengthen the legal status of IP rights.

As a result, the graffiti on the issue gets quite graphic at times.

Of course, most of it is on the virtual restrooms on the Internet, not so much the restrooms in the hotspots of San Jose's nightlife.* There'll be huge flamefests over some specific issue associated with intellectual property law, with people arguing everything from First Amendment rights to whether IP law might make open source development impossible sometime in the future.

And I find myself certifiably schizophrenic on the issue.

It's not that I don't have an opinion: I have very strong opinions on the worth of intellectual property, but they end up being on both sides of the argument. I can tell you, this can be very con-

---

*This, as anybody who lives in San Jose can tell you, is called IRONY. San Jose doesn't have nightlife. People living here drive to San Mateo if they actually want to have fun.

fusing. It means that I end up arguing both sides. And I think this is because there really *are* two sides to intellectual property, and they share nothing but the name.

To many people, including me, intellectual property is all about human inventiveness, about the very thing that makes us *humans* instead of animals (that, and thumbs, of course). And in that setting, the very name "intellectual property" is an affront: It's not property to be sold like chattel, it's the act of creation, it's the greatest thing any human can ever do. It's Art, with a capital A. It's the Mona Lisa, but it's also the end result of a long night of programming, and it's an end result that you as a programmer are damned *proud* of. It's something so precious that selling it isn't even possible: It's indelibly a part of who you are.

That kind of creativity—whether it be in the form of painting, music, sculpture, writing, or programming—should be sacred. The creator and the thing he or she created have a bond that cannot be severed. It's like the bond between a mother and child, or between bad Chinese food and MSG. But at the same time it's something that everybody in the whole world should be able to be part of, because it *is* humanity.

And then, in the other corner, weighing in at an approximate seven gadzillion billion U.S. dollars a year, intellectual property is huge business. Human creativity got a price tag, and it turned out to be quite expensive. Creativity is rare, and as a result it is not just expensive but also extremely lucrative. Which brings in a totally different class of arguments, and totally different kinds of people. The kind of people who call the end result of human creativity "property." Not to mention, of course, lawyers.

Read the title of this chapter again. The "property" people are winning. After all, their name stuck. So what's the problem?

The most well-known example of intellectual property is the notion of copyright. Copyrights are basically the codification of the rights of any creator to do with his or her creation as he or she wishes. The "owner" of the creation can decide on how that creation should be used.

Copyrights are also legally very simple to get. You don't have to register your copyright: You are automatically the copyright holder of whatever creative work you do. This is an important distinction from most other intellectual property law, mainly because it actually makes it easy for individuals, not just big corporations, to own copyrights. *You* can own a copyright, simply by virtue of writing, painting, or generally creating something unique. If you want to, you can add a legend like "(C) Copyright 2000 Yourname Here," but quite frankly, you don't need to. You own the copyright whether you say so or not. Saying so just makes it easier for other people to track you down if they want to use your work.

Of course, just owning a copyright in itself is not very useful. But the fact that you own what you create means that you can control how it is used. You have, for example, the right to sell such a work of art to somebody else, and nobody but the IRS gets to have any say in the matter. But it's about *more* than just the money, and that's where a lot of people seem to find themselves flummoxed.

For example, you can use your power as owner of a copyright to try to do more interesting things than just sell it. You can license it. This is even *better* than selling it; instead of selling the work of art you can sell the license to do certain things to it, and still retain the copyright on it. Basically, you can have your cake and eat it, too. This is how the Microsofts of the world get created: endlessly selling the rights to use something, without actually losing anything. No wonder people just *love* to own this kind of property.

Does anybody perhaps start to see a problem here? If you don't see anything strange so far, I have a bridge and a few pieces of waterfront property to sell you.

The basic problem with intellectual property is starting to show itself: You as the owner of intellectual property can effectively sell it forever, without ever losing anything yourself. You don't risk anything, and in fact you might decide to write your license in a way that basically says that even if the property is *flawed*, you cannot be held responsible in any way. Sounds preposterous? You'd be surprised.

Flaw: no consumer protection.

It gets worse. The copyright holder not only has the right to sell his or her property without losing it, but also the right to sue people who sell property that *looks* like his or hers. Clearly the copyright owner has rights over that *derived work*.

Clearly? Not so fast. Where do you draw the line between inspiration and copying? And what happens when different people come up with similar ideas? Who gets the gravy train of being able to sell his idea over and over and over again, and gets to tell the other people to butt out of his business? It's not just consumers who aren't protected, it's also *other* creative people who are not protected by the notion of "intellectual property."

What makes the discussion ugly at this point is that a lot of the arguments for stronger intellectual property rights are based on the notion of giving inventors and artists more "protection." What people don't seem to ever realize is that giving such powerful rights to some people also ends up taking rights away from others.

And maybe not so surprisingly, the proponents of stricter intellectual property laws are the organizations that stand to gain the most. Not the artists and inventors themselves, but the clearinghouses of IP: companies that make a living off other people's creativity. Oh, and lawyers, of course. The end result? Copyright law amendments like the infamous Digital Millennium Copyright Act (DMCA), which removes the last vestiges of consumer rights over the use of copyrighted material.

Now, if you are getting the notion that I think copyrights are actually detrimental, you're wrong. I happen to absolutely love copyrights, I just don't believe in taking the rights of the authors *too* far. Not to the point of screwing the consumer over. And I say this not just as a consumer, but as a producer of copyrighted material myself, both in the form of this book and of Linux itself.

I, as a copyright holder, have my rights. But with rights

come obligations—or as they say in certain neighborhoods, *noblesse oblige*. And so I have the obligation to use those rights in responsible ways, and not as a weapon against others who lack such rights. As one great American once declared, "Ask not what your copyright can do for you, ask what you can do for your copyright"—or something to that effect.

And in the end, copyright is, despite even the DMCA, a fairly mild and well-behaved form of intellectual property. The notion of "fair use" does still exist, and holding a copyright does not give *all* rights to the work to the copyright holder.

The same cannot be said for patents, trademarks, and trade secrets; the heavy drugs of IP. Discussions over software patents in particular have gotten so inflamed in technical circles that it officially counts as one of the subjects you should not discuss in polite company, along with gun control, abortion rights, medical marijuana, and whether Pepsi tastes better than Coca Cola. And the reason is that patents, in many ways, give control over new inventions similar to that of copyrights, but with few of the redeeming qualities of copyrights.

One of the most awkward issues with patents is that, unlike with copyrights, you don't get a patent just for inventing something new. No, you get a patent after you've gone through the painful and prolonged process of filing for it with the patent office. Waiting for the patent office, by the way, is a bit like standing in line at the DMV, but you have to realize that you stand in line with about twelve patent lawyers, and the line is TWO YEARS LONG. In short, it's not something you do for fun on a Friday evening if the kids fell asleep early.

As if to add insult to injury, the patent office doesn't necessarily have the resources to check whether the patent for a new invention of yours is really all that groundbreaking. It's not as if they have Einsteins* working for them, so it's fairly hard to give

---

*Actually, Einstein *did* work for the patent office when he did his work on special relativity. But he was special. Even most patent clerks admit that.

new inventions their proper checking. Which means that, in many cases, obviously bogus patents have been accepted. Think of it as the post office with Ph.D.'s—minus the guns.

So what's the result? Very few individuals get patents, for obvious reasons. *Companies,* on the other hand, get a ton of them. They are useful as weapons against other companies that threaten to sue over the patents *they* own. The patent system of today is basically a Cold War with IP instead of nukes. And it's not much prettier. The people left huddling in bomb shelters are the individual inventors, who have to deal with a system gone crazy and who lack the resources to have 12,000 lawyers on staff.

Now, if you want to avoid the bother with patents, you can go for the strongest drugs of IP, trade secrets. The advantage of the trade secret is that you don't have to worry about a Trade Secret Office or anything at all: You can just stamp your intellectual property "secret" and be done with it. You can still tell people about it, but you have to tell them it's a secret.

People used to do this all the time before, and that is actually why patent law was originally introduced. In order to encourage individuals and companies to expose their secrets, patent law allowed for protection in the marketplace for some time *if you divulged what your secret to success was.* A basic form of tit-for-tat: You tell how you do something, and we'll give you exclusive rights for X years.

Before patents, people would guard their technological advantage jealously and take their secrets to the grave. That was, for obvious reasons, bad for technical evolution because promising technologies were never divulged to anybody else. The promise of exclusive rights made patents a very powerful incentive to tell all, as you no longer had to worry about your competition finding out what you were doing—at which point you would otherwise have lost the protection of it being secret.

However, that was then, and this is now. These days even trade secrets have legal protection, for unfathomable reasons. Any sane person realizes that once a secret is out, it is no longer a secret. Except in the strange and twisty passages of intellectual property law, where secrets can continue to be secrets even after everybody knows what they are. And where the knowledge you have in your head can get you sued, if you happen to go to work for the wrong employer. Some intellectual property law is downright scary.

To a large degree, finding peace in this intellectual property war is what open source is all about. While a lot of people have their own opinions about what open source really tries to do, in many ways you can see it as a high-tech détente, a defusing of copyright as a weapon in this fight of intellectual property.

So open source would rather use the legal weapon of copyright as an invitation to join in the fun, rather than as a weapon against others. It's still the same old mantra: Make Love, Not War, except on a slightly more abstract level (probably a *lot* more abstract, considering some of the geeks I know).

But as with any major philosophical rift, there is always the other side of the story. This is where my certifiable schizophrenia comes in.

I've tried to explain why a lot of people feel that intellectual property, and especially the strengthening of intellectual property laws, is downright evil. Many in the open source community (and outside too, in all honesty) would like nothing better than to tear down all the nukes altogether, and totally abolish the Cold War of knowledge. Others disagree.

The other side of the picture is that yes, intellectual property may be unfair, and yes, intellectual property laws are largely designed to further the aims of large corporations over the rights of consumers or even the individual author or inventor. But boy is it *lucrative!* It concentrates the power of the powerful, and the very fact that it's a powerful weapon makes it so effective in the marketplace. The same reason that made nuclear weapons the ultimate force in the Cold War makes intellectual property so attractive in the war of technology. And technology sells.

And it also generates a very powerful positive-feedback cycle. Because intellectual property is such a good source of revenue, a lot of money is being spent on creating *more* intellectual property. And that very fact is important. In the same ways that wars have historically always been a source of invention and great leaps in engineering (initially, the computer itself was largely developed for purely military purposes), the virtual war of intellectual property rights helps feed the engine and brings never-before-seen resources into technology development. This is a good thing.

Of course, I, as an intellectual snob, am convinced that merely throwing resources around is not really all that conducive to true creativity. Just look at the music business of today. Kajillions of dollars are spent every year on finding the next hot artist—yet nobody really thinks that the Spice Girls (who have been richly rewarded for their contributions to their art) can compare to Wolfgang Amadeus Mozart (who died destitute). So throwing money at the problem does not make for that kind of genius.

But intellectual snobbism—the you-can't buy-a-genius philosophy—doesn't really work as a long-term business model. The creative juices are just so unpredictable, so hard to court on finding, that any long-term planning should not concentrate on the promise of pure genius. The technology development of today (and, sadly, the music) depends not on the Einsteins (and Mozarts) but on a huge army of plodding engineers (and, in the case of music, well-endowed young females) who may show only occasional flashes of brilliance. The added resources do not make for great art, but for slow and steady progress. And, in the end, this is all to the best.

The notion of plodding engineers may have less romantic appeal than the eccentric-genius approach. Just think about how many "Mad Scientist" movies there are compared to the number of "Plodding Engineer" movies. However, when it comes down to business, you do want your occasional flashes of genius but, even more than that, you want the steady stream of small improvements over time.

And this is where the power of intellectual property shines: Having grown so lucrative, it has become the holy grail of modern technology companies, feeding this big machine. And thus, thanks to IP protections the steady progress goes on, unhindered. It may not be all that creative any more, but it's dependable.

So I see both sides—although I have to admit that most of the time I'd rather see a more fun and inspiring world of technology. One where economic factors wouldn't *always* prevail. I have a dream—one day IP laws will be dictated by morals, not on who gets the biggest piece of the cake.

Trust me, I understand the economic issues. At the same time, I can't help but wish they did not have such an overwhelmingly negative impact on modern intellectual property law. The economic incentives to strengthen the ownership of intellectual property, and the difficulty in expressing the notion of "fair use" and "morals" in legal text, have caused the two viewpoints on IP to grow further apart. As in a dispute between two neighbors, neither side is willing to even acknowledge that the right solution is likely to be somewhere in between the two extremes.

Clearly, as the unfortunate passing of the DMCA showed, economic incentives are doing well. The question is, what kind of intellectual property law would help drive development while being less driven by crass money-grabbing interests?

The issue is intensified by the fact that modern technology (and the Internet in particular) are weakening many of the traditional forms of intellectual property protection almost faster than we can keep up. And in ways nobody could have predicted. Who would have imagined that Midwestern grandmothers would be pirating needlepoint instructions over the Internet? The ability to copy works of art—and technology itself—on a large scale has become so widespread and easily available that institutions with vested IP are running around doing the best they can to shore up their interests. They are doing all they can to make such copying illegal, and introducing new measures to actually outlaw technology that can be used for piracy.

What's wrong with this picture? The problem is that a lot of the new efforts to make it harder to illegally use other people's intellectual property also make it much harder to use other people's work in legal ways. The classic example of this from the Linux world is the so-called DeCSS lawsuit.

In the DeCSS suit, people who were working on technology to decode DVD movies were sued by the entertainment industry for making the code available to others on the Internet. It didn't matter to the judge on the case that the ultimate aim of the project was perfectly legal; the fact that the project could *potentially* be used for illegal purposes made it illegal in the United States to distribute even the information on where to find the instructions to do the decoding. (The "DeCSS" name itself comes from the project undoing the DVD Content Scrambling System—CSS. So you "de-CSS" something in order to remove the scrambling so that you can watch the movie on your computer.)

This is a perfect example of intellectual property law being used not to help foster innovation, but to control the marketplace, to control what consumers can and cannot do. It's an example of intellectual property law gone bad.

Such misuses of intellectual property power aren't limited to technology, by the way. Another classic example is the use of trade secret law to prosecute and persecute the people who tried to inform the public about Scientology. The Church of Scientology successfully claimed that their scriptures ("Advanced Technology") fell under trade secret protection, and used IP law to defend them from being made public.

What are the alternatives? Imagine an intellectual property

law that actually took *other* people's rights into account, too. Imagine IP laws that encouraged openness and sharing. Laws that say sure, you can still have your secrets, whether they be technological or religious, but that doesn't *mandate* legal protection for such secrecy.

Yeah, I know. How unrealistic of me.

An End to Control

The way to survive and flourish is to make the best damn product you can. And if you can't survive and flourish on that, then you shouldn't. If you can't make a good car, then you deserve to go down like the rock that was the U.S. auto industry in the 1970s. Success is about quality and about giving folks what they want.

It's not about trying to control people.

The trouble is, people and companies are too often motivated by pure greed. And that always causes them to lose in the long run. Greed leads to decisions governed by paranoia and a need for total control. Those are bad, short-sighted decisions that end up in disaster, or near disaster. The simple example on everyone's mind has been the phenomenal early success of wireless technology in Europe at the expense of American companies. While the U.S. companies individually tried to control the market by using their own proprietary standards, the European companies rallied around a single standard, GSM, and chose to compete based on which company could produce the best product and provide the best service. The U.S. companies have fallen behind, plagued by their own competing standards. With a market buoyed by a common standard, the European companies have all shared in the boom. That's why kids in Prague were swapping cell-phone text messages years before kids in Peoria had even heard about it as a new way of cheating on tests.

If you try to make money by controlling a resource, you'll eventually find yourself out of business. This is a form of despotism, and history overflows with examples of its ill effects. Say it's the 1800s in the U.S. West and you control the source of water for local farmers. You're stingy with the water and overcharge. At some point, it inevitably becomes profitable for someone else to devise a way to bring it in from somewhere else, and then your market collapses. Or technology advances so that pipes can transport water, from a distance. Either way, as circumstances change your hold gets broken and you're left with nothing. This happens all the time, and it's amazing that people still can't see it coming.

Flash forward to the music industry in the waning years of the twentieth century. The resource it controls is entertainment. A company owns the rights to an artist's work. That artist produces a number of successful singles, but the company puts maybe one or two of those singles on each CD it produces. That way it can sell multiple CDs, instead of the one that everyone wants. Then somebody invents the technology for MP3. Suddenly, music can be downloaded from the Internet. MP3 is about doing the right thing for consumers by giving them a choice.

So if a typical CD costs $10 and contains two singles a consumer wants, it may make more sense for him to purchase those singles separately—along with others he wants—off MP3 for $1.50 apiece. No longer is the buyer trapped in a despotic situation, living by the greed-inspired rules of the music company, which wants to give up just the bite-sized pieces that it chooses to give up. There's a good reason why the music industry is scared to death of MP3 and its sister technologies, Napster and Gnutella. The price of water got so high that it became profitable for somebody to devise a new method of bringing it in from somewhere else.

But this is an industry with a history of trying to control consumers—if not by what music it chooses to release, then by copyright and technology. This is the industry that tripped all over itself in the 1960s, trying to keep consumers from copying music onto tapes when that technology entered the market. Because the industry felt tapes were the perfect medium for people to disobey copyright laws, it argued for ways to protect its copyrights. This was a bad excuse. The industry was taking the moral high ground and pleading copyright when it was simply trying to maintain control of its niche franchise. The fact is, tapes never hurt the music industry. Sure, people copied music for their own use, but that only meant that people actually bought more LPs from which to copy. Duh. A few decades later, when CDs came out, the players were built so that you couldn't copy your tape perfectly. Paranoia strikes again. Next came digital tapes. They involved a different sampling rate from CDs—48 kilohertz versus 44.1—to prevent users from copying their CDs onto digital tape. Again the industry tried to screw over the customer to get control. But in the case of digital tapes, the market never quite hit. It was a bit like fooling with Mother Nature.

By trying to control each successive technology, the music industry only helps inspire people to devise new ways around it. Are they ever going to get it?

That brings us, inevitably, to DVDs. This time the entertainment industry delivered much better sound and video than VHS tapes, plus a smaller format and greater ease-of-use. But they added encryption to prevent copying. And to add insult to injury, they added geographic area codes. The DVD you bought at the San Francisco airport wouldn't play in Europe. It made a perverse sense to the industry: Hey you guys, we can sell movies at a higher price in Europe! So let's make sure that Europeans can't buy movies from the United States.

Could the entertainment industry not have predicted the obvious? That the price of water would get so high that somebody would devise a new method of piping it in from somewhere else?

Yes, while the industry was greedily trying to control people through technology, the DVD encryption was cracked—not even by people who wanted to copy DVDs but by people who simply wanted to view them under Linux. These are folks who actually wanted to *buy* DVDs, but they couldn't; the discs would have been useless on their equipment. The industry's moves to protect its fiefdom backfired: It simply prevented the market from expanding, and created the incentive for the cracking of the DVD encryption.

Once again, the short-term strategy turned out to be the wrong thing to do.

The entertainment industry is just one example. The same thing has been happening for years in software. That's why Microsoft's strategy of bundling software is ultimately doomed to fail. Open source products, on the other hand, cannot possibly be used in a despotic manner because they're free. If somebody tried to bundle things with Linux, somebody else could just unbundle it and sell it the way people really want it.

It's doubly futile to attempt to control people through technology. In the end, it always not only hurts the company but also hinders the acceptance of the technology. A recent example is Java, which has lost a lot of the appeal it originally had. By trying to control the Java environment, Sun Microsystems basically lost it. Java is still doing reasonably well, but it surely hasn't lived up to its potential.

Sun wasn't trying to make money on Java itself, but the company saw the programming language as a way to make its computer more unique to users and get us out of Microsoft's grip—and sell more Sun hardware, by the way. But while they weren't really trying to make money on Java, they did feel that they had to keep control of it as a phenomenon and as a microbe. All of their licensing terms came with a lot of extra baggage just for this control.

Good product. But the problem was that they were trying too hard to screw over Microsoft. They were motivated by fear, loathing, and hate, which is sort of a mid-to-late 1990s approach to business. (Think of the Grateful Dead lyric: "Ain't no time to hate.") And because they were so hateful of Microsoft and so afraid, they made all the wrong licensing decisions. They made it difficult for everybody, even their partners, to use the product. That's why companies like Hewlett Packard and IBM all eventually decided to make their own Java implementations. They just said "Screw Sun."

Sun tried to get Java standardized through two different standardization bodies, and each time they basically pulled out because of the control issues. On the one hand, Sun wanted to standardize the language. But at the same time they didn't want to lose control. So the standardization boards basically said, "Hey, this is not just about you." And as a result, Sun just flaked out. It's an example of a company trying to control technology in ways that make no sense for the people who actually use the technology. And it's always going to fail for the company. It also makes the technology itself fail—or take longer to be accepted.

Contrast that with the If-you-love-something-set-it-free strategy taken by Palm Computing. The folks at Palm made their development environment open, and also opened up their platform, not only to vendors but to individuals who would want to write programs for the platform. They opened up their APIs and made it easy to get their development tools for free. What this did was create a cottage industry around the Palm Pilot. It made the Palm phenomenon more than just one company struggling in a new market. So now you have companies selling games that work on Palm Pilots, and more advanced calendar programs than what Palm itself offers. Now the consumer can choose what he or she wants and everybody benefits, particularly Palm, which enjoys a larger market as a result of opening itself up.

Handspring is doing the same thing with its device, the Visor. It's a Palm competitor that uses the Palm operating system, and the company takes openness a step further by allowing hardware plug-ins like GPS receivers and mobile phone attachments. Like Palm, Handspring is creating a community of companies to support a new platform.

What Sun could have done is allow anybody to do their own Java—no strings attached—while wagering that they themselves could do a better job. That's the sign of a company that isn't blinded by greed or by fear of competition. It's the sign of a company that believes in itself. And doesn't have time to hate.

THE AMUSEMENT RIDE AHEAD

Is there anything more obnoxious than business prognosticators? Those self-important types who pretend to know where the insane technology amusement ride will take us? I guess they serve a good function. They populate the panel discussions and keynote speeches of the indistinguishable technology conferences that seem to crop up like unpleasant, inedible mushrooms in your flower bed. People hoping to cash in on technology trends spend thousands of dollars to hear them speak at technology conferences. It keeps an army of hotel workers and food handlers and bartenders honestly employed, so I suppose they serve a purpose.

And now David tells me that I should do one of those "Future of Business" chapters, too. I feel a bit sullied by the thought, but hey, he didn't let me drown while we were boogey-boarding, and if he believes that readers will think the future of business is more interesting than the meaning of life, then I'll just shut up and write.

However.

I'll go on record saying that I've not been a very good predictor of much of anything in my life, as far as I can remember. Did I predict that the little operating system I started writing for my own use would someday be all over the place? Nope. Took me by surprise, it did. My only defense is that nobody else seems to do be doing any better on this crystal ball thing either, and if I was taken by surprise by how big Linux became in the industry, then everybody else was absolutely flabbergasted. So I probably did better than most. And who knows? Maybe through this chapter I will be known as the Nostradamus of our time.

And maybe not. Here goes, anyway.

We can, of course, look to past experience. We can trace in sad detail how, say, an invincible-seeming company like AT&T went limp—and we can predict that if we stick around long enough, the weeds will overrun those tidy little green buildings in Redmond someday, too. Just as today's hot young starlet will develop wrinkles and sagging breasts, today's business hero will be supplanted by a new, more inspired model; and the hero's company, even if it breaks a sweat reinventing itself—or whatever they're calling it this month—will end up sagging and groaning, AT&T-style.

Call it evolution. It's certainly not rocket science. No business will live forever, and that is just as well.

But what is it that actually drives this evolution? Is there some fundamental, inherent evolution of technology that will one day cause computers to take over, leaving the human race behind in the dust, like some people seem to think? Or is it just some random inevitability of progress, a "straight ahead and damn the torpedoes" kind of thing that causes technological advances?

I say no.

Technology is what we make of it, and neither business nor technology will change the basic nature of human needs and yearnings. As with everything else, the evolution slowly but inexorably will cause technology to move away from plain survival through a society based on communication and finally into the realm of entertainment (*déjà vu* alert: Yes, you've seen this theory before in these pages, and, assuming you stick around to the bitter end, you'll see it once more).

Humans are destined to be party animals, and technology will follow.

So forget all the predictions about what technology can do in ten years. That's not very relevant at all. We were able to put a man on the moon thirty years ago, and we've not been back since. I'm personally convinced that is simply because the moon turned out to be a drab place with basically no night-life at all—sort of like San Jose. As a result, people didn't *want* to go back, and the amount of technology we've amassed in the meantime doesn't mean a thing. The moon stays empty.

What really matters when you talk about the future of technology is what people *want*. Once you've figured that out, the only remaining question is how quickly you can mass-produce the thing and make it cheap enough that people can get it without sacrificing anything *else* they want. Nothing else really matters.

A small digression is in order here. What really sells, of course, is *perception*, not reality. Cruise liners sell the perception of freedom, of the salty seas, of good food and romance of *Love Boat* proportions. Who cares if the cabin is cramped if you *feel* like you're free as a bird!

And what does this all means? It explains, for example, why people are going so ga-ga over the Sony PlayStation 2, the single biggest piece of technology to hit the store shelves this year. (I'm writing this just days after it was introduced in the United States in late October 2000). Talk about the embodiment of the entertainment society!

It also points out how personal computers have a perception problem. Clearly the PC industry is nervous about game consoles, mainly because they are seen as nonthreatening, fun and cheap, while PC's are mostly seen as complicated and expensive. Sometimes even inimical.

It also makes me personally convinced that if we're still talking in a big way about operating systems fifteen years from now, something is seriously wrong somewhere. This may sound strange coming from somebody whose main claim to fame is writing his own operating system, but the fact is that, statistically speaking, *nobody* wants an operating system.

In fact, nobody even wants a computer. What everybody wants is this magical toy that can be used to browse the Web, write term papers, play games, balance the checkbook, and so on.

The fact that you need a computer and an operating system to do all this is something that most people would rather not ever think about.

This is why a lot of analysts like the notion of devices like the Sony PlayStation 2 that take over a number of the chores of a computer, without having that scary hand-sweat-producing property of being obviously complicated, scary machines. Which is technologically senseless, as we're getting more and more computers into the house all the time like this, while being *unaware* of how complicated and scary they could be.

So my bet for the next Microsoft would be Sony, if they can just get all the pieces lined up properly. Now I'm not claiming that this is a prediction of Nostradamus-like mindbogglingness (yes, I know that's probably not a real word, but it *should* be). There are others who would agree with this, but I'm trying to articulate *why* it is happening.

Not that I'm predicting the demise of the PC, like many have unsuccessfully done before. The fundamental strengths of PCs are still there; they are the Swiss army knife of computers. Overtly complicated enough to scare off people who don't like technology—complicated exactly *because* they are not tailor-made for only one thing. That flexibility becomes the very thing that makes them attractive.

And then, the one ring to rule them all, and in the darkness bind them: communication. Everywhere. You can't live without checking email at least twice an hour? No problem, my email-addicted friend. You can have the slightly guilty feeling of taking the day off at the beach, yet always be in touch with what's going on at work. Remember: What sells is not the *reality* of being on vacation, but the *perception* of freedom. Size does matter after all, if only to make all of the technological wonders seem trivial and nonthreatening.

And where is Linux itself, and open source generally, in all this? You won't even know. It will be inside those Sony machines. You'll never see it, you'll never know it, but it's there, making it all run. It will be in that cell phone, which is at the same time acting as your very own personal communications hub for the rest of your electronic widgets when you're away from your wireless local area network.

You'll see. It's only a matter of time. And money.

WHY OPEN SOURCE MAKES SENSE

IBM is a company with a history of screwing people over. It made its money by getting a captive audience and making sure nobody else got a foothold. That's how most computer companies worked, in fact. It's how some of them still do. Then, when IBM developed the personal computer, it unintentionally opened up its technology for anyone to replicate. That single act did more than anything to spur the PC Revolution, which has in turn spurred the Information Revolution, Internet Revolution, New Economy—whatever it is they're now calling the massive changes taking place throughout the world.

It's the best illustration of the limitless benefits to be derived from the open source philosophy. While the PC wasn't developed using the open source model, it is an example of a technology that was opened for any person or company to clone and improve and sell. In its purest form, the open source model allows anyone to participate in a project's development or commercial exploitation. Linux is obviously the most successful example. What started out in my messy Helsinki bedroom has grown to become the largest collaborative project in the history of the world. It began as an ideology shared by software developers who believed that computer source code should be shared freely, with the General Public License—the anticopyright—as the movement's powerful tool. It evolved to became a method for the continuous development of the best technology. And it evolved further to gain widespread market acceptance, as seen in the snowballing adoption of Linux as an operating system for Web servers, and in its unexpectedly generous IPOs.

What was inspired by ideology has proved itself as technology and is working in the marketplace. Now open source is expanding beyond the technical and business domains. At Harvard University Law School, professors Larry Lessig (who is now at Stanford) and Charles Nesson have brought the open source model to law. They started the Open Law Project, which relies on volunteer lawyers and law students posting opinions and research to the project's Web site to help develop arguments and briefs challenging the United States Copyright Extension Act. The theory is that the strongest arguments will be developed when the largest number of legal minds are working on a project, and as a mountain of information is generated through postings and repostings. The site nicely sums up the tradeoff from the traditional approach: "What we lose in secrecy, we expect to regain in depth of sources and breadth of argument." (Put in another context: With a million eyes, all software bugs will vanish.)

It's a wrinkle on how academic research has been conducted for years, but one that makes sense on a number of fronts. Think of how this approach could speed up the development of cures for disease, for example. Or how, with the best minds on the task, international diplomacy could be strengthened. As the world becomes smaller, as the pace of life and business intensifies, and as the technology and information become available, people realize the tight-fisted approach is becoming increasingly outmoded.

The theory behind open source is simple. In the case of an operating system, the source code—the programming instructions underlying the system—is free. Anyone can improve it, change it, exploit it. But those improvements, changes, and exploitations have to be made freely available. Think Zen. The project belongs to no one and to everyone. When a project is opened up, there is rapid and continual improvement. With teams of contributors working in parallel, the results can happen far more speedily and successfully than if the work were being conducted behind closed doors.

That's what we experienced with Linux. Imagine: Instead of a tiny cloistered development team working in secret, you have a monster on your side. Potentially millions of the brightest minds are contributing to a project, and are supported by a peer-review process that has no, er, peer.

The first time people hear about the open source approach, it sounds ludicrous. That's why it has taken years for the message of its virtues to sink in. Ideology isn't what has sold the open source model. It started gaining attention when it was obvious that open source was the best method of developing and improving the highest quality technology. And now it is winning in the marketplace, an accomplishment has brought open source its greatest acceptance. Companies were able to be created around numerous value-added services, or to use open source as a way of making a technology popular. When the money rolls in, people get convinced.

One of the least understood pieces of the open source puzzle is how so many good programmers would deign to work for absolutely no money. A word about motivation is in order. In a society where survival is more or less assured, money is not the greatest of motivators. It's been well established that folks do their best work when they are driven by a passion. When they are having fun. This is as true for playwrights and sculptors and entrepreneurs as it is for software engineers. The open source model gives people the opportunity to live their passion. To have fun. And to work with the world's best programmers, not the few who happen to be employed by their company. Open source developers strive to earn the esteem of their peers. That's got to be highly motivating.

It seems that Bill Gates doesn't understand this. Is it possible that he's now embarrassed by an off-putting rhetorical question he asked in 1976? "One thing you do is prevent good software from being written. Who can afford to do professional work for nothing?" he wrote in a letter to open source programmers.

In fact, one way to understand the open source phenomenon is to think about how science was perceived by religion so many centuries ago (if not today, by some creatures). Science was originally viewed as something dangerous, subversive, and antiestablishment—basically how software companies sometimes view open source. And just as science wasn't born out of an effort to undermine the religious establishment, open source wasn't conceived in order to detonate the software establishment. It is there to produce the best technology, and to see where it goes.

Science on its own does not make money. It has been the secondary effects of science that create all the wealth. The same goes for open source. It allows the creation of secondary industries that challenge established businesses, much the way the spinoffs of science challenged the church. You find small companies like VA Linux taking advantage of open source and suddenly being able to compete with traditional corporations. In the words of Sir Isaac Newton, standing on the shoulders of giants.

And yes, as open source gains momentum in the world economy, and as its developers earn recognition, they are becoming increasingly bankable as employees. Companies search credit lists, which are traditionally appended to open source software contributions, to determine who is making multiple contributions. And then they instruct their human resources departments to deliver a wheelbarrow full of money and stock options to potential employees. In a previous paragraph I pronounced that money is not the greatest motivator, and, no, I haven't changed my mind in the ensuing sentences. But I must say that money isn't such a bad thing to have as a reward for hard work. It certainly is handy when it comes to filling up the gas tank in my BMW.

Like science itself, open source's secondary effects are endless. It is creating things that until recently were considered impossible, and opening up unexpected new markets. With Linux, as with other open source projects, companies can make their own versions and their own changes, which really isn't possible any other way. It's exciting to realize that just about everything that's ever been done with Linux was not remotely on the radar when we started. It is even taking off in China. Traditionally, software development in Asia has primarily been about translating American or European software. Now folks in that part of the world are using Linux to develop their own software. And I'm really proud of the guy who came up to me at Comdex and wanted to show me the gasoline pump that was running Linux. It was a prototype gasoline pump that was running Linux because he wanted to have Web browsers so gasoline customers could go to CNN.com during the three minutes they're waiting for their tanks to fill. Standing on the shoulders of giants.

It's inspiring that people are using technologies like Linux to just make a better gas pump. That sort of innovation is not likely to have happened within the confines of a company, because if you were a company taking Linux to market you would go for the obvious, which right now is the server market or the high-end desktop market. But open source in general allows companies to make their own decisions about what they want to do. So it's Linux in embedded devices. It's Tivo running Linux and the Transmeta Web Slate running Linux and Telephony using Linux. This is how billions of dollars in wealth is being created from open source.

It's like letting the universe take care of itself. By not controlling the technology, you are not limiting its uses. You make it available and people make local decisions—to use it as a launching pad for their own products and services. And while most of those decisions don't make sense in the larger scale of things, they actually work really well. This is not about trying to spread Linux. It's about making Linux available and then letting it spread itself. And this doesn't apply only to Linux. It applies to any project that's open.

Open source makes sense.

People don't quibble with the need for free speech. It is a liberty that people have defended with their lives. Freedom is always something you have to defend with your life. But it's also not an easy choice to make initially. And the same is true of openness. You just have to make the decision to be open. It's a difficult stance to take at first, but it actually creates more stability in the end.

Think of politics. If the logic that's used against open source were applied to government, then we would always have one-party rule. Obviously, a single-party rule is a great deal simpler than our system of multiple parties, the open political system in which much of the world operates. With one party you don't have to worry about getting agreement with other people. The reasoning would follow that government is too important to waste on the give-and-take of openness. For some reason people see the fallacy of this argument as it applies to politics and government, but not as it applies to business. Ironically, in business it makes people nervous.

The arguments a company uses to keep from opening up technology are convincing. *That's not how things are done,* management says. And it's scary. People are frightened of change, partly because they don't know how it is going to turn out. By sticking to the status quo, a company can make a better judgment of where it will go, and sometimes that seems more important than being hugely successful. These are companies that will be predictably successful instead of being unpredictably really, really, *really* successful.

It isn't easy for a corporation to turn an existing product into an open source product. There are a host of thorny issues. For one thing, over the course of months or years that it developed the product, the company built up a great deal of internal knowledge. This in-house intellectual property is the company's bread and butter. The organization is unwilling to relinquish the intellectual property that keeps it alive. But also, the very existence of this internal knowledge creates a barrier for outsiders. It discourages them from participating.

But I have seen companies make the move from closed to open. One story is Wapit, a Finnish company creating service and support infrastructure for various interactive devices. This project involved the company's wall-phone-style Web server. For them, the decision to open source their software makes perfect sense. They want to build up their service, but they have to build up their infrastructure first. That requires writing a lot of software. It's a necessary evil. So instead of viewing it as a decision to make its intellectual property available to others, they look at it this way: The writing of software takes a lot of engineering time, but it isn't something that creates value from being tightly held at the company.

There were a few things working in Wapit's favor. First, it was not a huge project. Second, the decision to open source was made in the early stages of the company's existence. Management reasoned that it had the resources in-house to develop the product, but it wanted to push to have something more than could be created in-house. It also determined that open sourcing is a good way of furthering Wap as a standard for others to work on.

Early in the game, the company asked for my advice and I told them they needed to fight the urge to have decisions made internally. I suggested that if they were having meetings in which decisions should be made, those meetings should not be closed to outsiders. By keeping the decision-making process a company affair, they would run the risk of alienating outsiders, who would have trouble getting past the company's Old Boy's network. That's one of the major problems of establishing and maintaining an open source project from a corporate environment. It's easy to give lip service to open source, but it can unintentionally degenerate into a two-tier society: Us vs. Them. A lot of decisions get made the easy way—sitting at the cafeteria table discussing the options and developing a consensus without ever opening up the discussion to the outside. People from the outside who have valid opinions are essentially voted down by the fact that the decision was already made in the company cafeteria.

This was one of the problems that plagued Netscape in the months following that company's much-heralded decision, in the spring of 1998, to release the source code (called Mozilla) for its next-generation browser. It took a long time before the project truly lived up to its open source promise. There was a camp of Netscape insiders who would not accept small patches from outsiders. Everybody inside knew each other, and if they weren't physically sitting around a coffee shop making decisions, there was a virtual coffee shop in which the insiders stayed fairly close. Instead of being seen as embarking on the first great experience in taking an existing commercial project and opening it up, Netscape generated a bit of bad press. When word of its inactivity got out, Netscape could no longer take the high moral ground. That helped them open up to outsiders. Now the project seems to be much more dynamic.

When folks first hear about the possibility of opening up an existing commercial project, they tend to ask the same questions. One question has to do with how people inside the company would feel about the possibility of having an outsider produce work that is better than their own—and having that so publicly noticeable. I think they should feel great about it, and great that they are getting paid for not even doing most of the work. In that regard, open source—or open *anything*, for that matter—is unforgiving. It shows who can get the job done, who is better. You can't hide behind managers.

Open source is the best way of leveraging outside talent. But you still need to have somebody inside the company who keeps track of the company's needs. That person may not even be the project's leader. In fact, it could be a benefit to the company if someone on the outside takes it over and is doing it for free. It's fine if someone outside is doing a better job. The trouble is, the outsider might lead the project in a direction that doesn't satisfy the company's requirements. So the company must take care of its own needs. The opening of the project might enable the organization to shrink its local resources, but that doesn't mean it can get rid of them. The project could expand to become far bigger than it would have been at a single company. Outside resources make for a cheaper, more complete, and more balanced system, but there's this flip side: The expanded system no longer takes only the *company's* needs into account. It actually might consider the needs of customers.

Probably the most vexing thing in the whole process is giving up control and just accepting the fact that outsiders may actually know better. The other difficulty is finding a strong technical leader in the company. This has to be somebody who is trusted by everyone on two levels—both a technical and a political level. It has to be someone who is able to acknowledge the fact that the project may have been flawed from the start. Instead of trying to hide from such problems, the leader must be able to convince everybody that the best thing to do is to go back and start over, which means breaking stuff. It's not a message people want to hear. However, coming from someone who commands respect, it's a message people will accept.

Given the nature of office politics and how corporations typically work, the technical lead person would have to be someone with a fairly strong personality. He or she should be somebody who likes working by email and who avoids taking sides. I wouldn't use the word "liaison," because that would imply there are two distinct sides here—the inside camp and the outside camp. And that's not the way it should be. This technical lead person gets paid by the company to do open source. He or she knows, and everybody else knows, that this person is not paid to agree with his counterparts in the company, but simply to do the project. There's a danger with having the leader too closely associated with the company. Folks might trust his or her technical ability, but not the nontechnical judgment.

Is there a diplomat in the house?

It's like "Find me one honest man."

This is why I have tried so hard over the years to avoid getting involved with Linux companies. This is becoming increasingly critical now that the money is materializing. With so many dollars floating around, people start questioning your motivations. For me, it's helpful that I've been known as being neutral. You have no idea how important it is to me to maintain that neutrality. It drives me nuts.

Okay. You're right, I should stop preaching. Open source is not for everyone or every project or every corporation. But the more that people start taking stock of the success of Linux, the more they realize this isn't the knee-jerk rantings of idealistic, unwashed high-schoolers.

Open up anything, and the possibilities will follow. I've been talking about open source for as long as journalists have been asking me about it, which is basically the last five years. It used to be that you had to explain and explain what's so great about it. And, frankly, it felt like an endless trek. It was like trudging in mud.

People get it now.

FAME AND FORTUNE

"What about the burden of fame?" That's what some people will ask me. And let me tell you, the "burden" is not a burden at all. It's fun being famous, and famous people who say otherwise are just trying to be nice and make nonfamous people feel like they're better off. You're supposed to be humble about your fame, and complain about how it destroys your life.

But face it, everybody dreams of fame and riches. I know I did. As a teenager I wished to become a famous scientist. Albert Einstein, but better. Who doesn't? If not a scientist, then a racecar driver. Or a rock star. Or Mother Teresa. Or the President of the United States.

And actually, getting there was not at all painful. Sure, I may not be Albert Einstein but I feel comfortable about having actually made a difference, and about doing something meaningful. And getting recognized for it makes the whole thing all the better. So the next time you hear somebody complaining about fame and riches, ignore them. They're just doing it because it's what you're supposed to do.

So is it all good? Of course not. There are certainly downsides to being well-known. I don't have people recognize me in the streets (or at least not very often), but the huge amount of email I get is interspersed with the occasional message that is really hard to answer, and also hard to ignore. What do you say to somebody who asks you to give the eulogy for his dad that you never met? I never replied to that email, and I still feel a bit guilty about it. That was a very important thing for somebody, and to me it ended up being just an inconvenience.

Or how do you tell somebody who asks you to give a keynote speech at a conference that you really don't have the time or the inclination? How do you make people realize that you long ago stopped listening to phone-mail messages, without appearing to be an inconsiderate bastard? Which you really are, after all. It's not as if I end up caring all that deeply about every issue, just because I care deeply about the issue I'm known for: Linux.

Of course, eventually it becomes really easy to just say no. Or ignore the requests entirely; one of the reasons I love email is that it's so convenient and easy to ignore—what's one more email in the few hundred I get every day? The medium is so far removed from the person that it very seldom gets personal enough to make you feel guilty about ignoring it. It happens (see above), but it doesn't happen very often. And even when you don't ignore it, saying "no" over email is a lot easier to do than in person or over the phone.

The problem is fundamentally one of the expectations people end up having about well-known people. And the fact that it's obviously not possible to live up to all the expectations—while feeling like you should at least try to do so. That's partly what made writing this book a pretty nerve-wracking experience—trying to write a reasonably personal book, while at the same time not really disappointing people who expected something different.

And some of the expectations are downright silly. I often get the feeling that some people expect me to be a modern-day monk—living a frugal life in solitude. All because I thought that making Linux open and freely available on the Internet was a good idea, and because I didn't take the traditional commercial approach to software. So then I get self-conscious and rather defensive about the fact that I actually enjoy spending money, and that I've finally upgraded my old Pontiac Grand Am to something more fun.*

Which brings up the second question after the "burden of fame" one. Namely, "Will success spoil Linus (and/or Linux)?" Will I turn into a self-centered spoiled brat who writes books about himself because he likes seeing his name in print, and because it pays off his new useless car?

The answer, of course, is yes.

After all, take a person whose life-long philosophy has been to have fun and do something interesting, then add some money and fame, and what do you expect will happen? Instant philanthropist? I don't think so. Giving away money to charity really never even entered my mind until David actually asked the question during the making of this book. I looked at him blankly. "Shave the whales" was the first thing that came to my mind. Obviously I was not born to have great financial responsibility.

Does success change how you think about things? It does. Linux was a different animal when there were just fifty very technical users, as opposed to 25 million (or whatever the number is today) normal people who use it at least occasionally. And Linux was very different back when the only people working on it were people who did it entirely because it was fun and interesting—with none of the commercial interests that are so obviously there today.

And the same is true of Linus the person. Things change, and claiming that this isn't so doesn't change the facts. Linux is not the same movement it was five years ago, and Linus isn't the same person he was back then. And part of what has made doing Linux

*There's nothing wrong with a Pontiac Grand Am, and it's a fine car. It's also probably the most "average Joe" car in the whole United States, and some journalists have found it interesting that I would have such an embarrassingly regular car. It's not even Japanese, for chrissake! People will lose all respect for me when I admit that I spent hours agonizing over the exact color of my new car—a much less practical BMW Z3. Remember—"Just for Fun." That car is completely and utterly useless for anything *but* fun. And that's just the way I like it.

so very interesting to me has been exactly the fact that it hasn't been the same, and that new issues have continuously kept coming up. And they haven't been just technological issues, but issues involving how the whole meaning of Linux changes in the face of success. Life would be boring otherwise.

So instead of using the word "spoiled," I'd prefer to just say that commercial success has made both Linux and me "different." I'd hesitate to say "grown up"—I think, for me, having three kids made far more of a difference that way—but simply different. Better, in many ways, but also less pure. Linux used to be *just* for technical people, and a safe haven for geeks. A bastion of purity, where technology mattered and little else.

These days that is not true anymore. Linux still has the strong technical background, but having millions of users makes everybody very aware of the fact that you have to be a lot more careful about what you do. Backward compatibility is suddenly a factor—and some day, twenty years from now, somebody will come along, say that enough is enough, and start his own operating system called "Fredix."* Without all the historical baggage. And that's exactly as it should be.

But what makes me inordinately proud is that even when "Fredix" comes along, things won't be the same anymore. If nothing else, what Linux has done is to make people aware of a new way of doing things, of how open source actually enables people to build on the work done by others. Open source has been around for a long time, but what Linux did was to move it into the general consciousness. So when Fredix comes along, it won't have to start from scratch.

And thus, the world has become a slightly better place.

---

*Or "Diannix," as the case may be. In another twenty years, hopefully computer science will have progressed past the current male-dominated scene it is now. . . .

*Nearly a year after we started working on this book, Linus and I paid
a Friday night visit to the car racing/batting cage place where we had
competed with each other months earlier. This time, Linus clobbered me at
both activities: He drove faster and made better hits. Later, over Turkish
food, I blamed my lousy performance on a particularly frustrating day at
work.*

*He looked up and said: "Well, you've got to hang in there for three
more months."*

"Why?"

"Isn't that when you vest your first chunk of stock options?"

*The reason I bring this up is because the night of our previous
competition at the car racing/batting cage place, Linus confessed that
because of his poor memory, he regularly had to ask Tove to remind him
of his phone numbers. Suddenly he now remembers somebody else's vesting
schedule, and he can rattle off where we were when I first mentioned it
to him. A year ago he seemed to delight in the role of an absent-minded
professor, fuzzy about the details of anything less significant than Super-
String Theory or the memory capacity of his earliest computers. Now he is
incredibly tuned in.*

*Back in January we sat in my old hot tub and I joked about the
Marin Historical Commission bugging me to donate it to their museum.
In August he casually says, "Hey, when are you going to donate that hot
tub?" He doesn't have to consult an electronic device to remember the dates
when Avuton will be visiting. He is plugged into the personal details of
friends and co-workers in a way he didn't seem to be a year earlier. In*

fact, he even knows what's going on with my friends and co-workers. And for a fellow whose first words to me on the subject were, "Actually, I don't remember much of my childhood," he suddenly seems to have conjured up the memories: "Did I tell you how embarrassed I was when my mother wanted me to ask my grandfather to give me the extra 100 FM I needed to buy my first watch?"

The clarity thing was just one way Linus seemed to have changed over the course of an important year in his life. There were little things. In November, we took the family road trip to Los Angeles that provided the backdrop for the "Meaning of Life" preface, partly because the Torvaldses were invited to stay at the Brentwood home of the Finnish Consulate General. Before the trip, Linus was glazed-eyed as he scanned the wine counter of a Santa Clara Safeway. "Help me pick out wine as a gift," he said. "I know nothing about wine." Ten months later he knows which of two similar cabernets we should choose from the Bodega Bay Lodge minibar, to drink while watching an in-room action movie. I catch him swirling his wine before drinking.

And then there's the exercise thing. On my first visit to Linus's home, he seemed to have a typical geek-like cavalier approach to his body and physical well-being, the "my-body's-just-there-to-carry-around-my-brilliant-mind" philosophy. Linus even seemed to take pride in the fact that he never exercised. Tove obviously felt differently. Her karate trophies lined a full bookcase, and her aerobics videos rested on the television set. And it seemed to be a point of contention. "Maybe in five years some doctor will tell me I'll have to lose weight or something," Linus said at the time.

I like to exercise and figured it should be a main component of our outings. I wanted to introduce him to surfing, but it made sense to start out with boogie-boarding. We drove over to Half Moon Bay one afternoon in early May, rented wet suits and boards, and Linus protested heavily at the thought of wading into the chilly waters of the Pacific, even in a wet suit. But within minutes something amazing happened: He delighted in riding the waves. "This is great," he enthused like a five-year old at one point, slapping me a high five. Of course, about fifteen minutes later he developed a nasty leg cramp—from being so out of shape, he reasoned— and had to stop. (When the cramp hit, he just sat there in the white water, apparently unable to get up, as waves washed over him. My first thought was: "Oh fuck. If I kill this guy, I'll have millions of nerds on my case.")

He looked forward to everything we did during the reporting phase of this book: playing tennis, racing each other at swimming, doing the scary amusements at Great America, driving golf balls. It got to the point at which he became less interested in sitting around talking into my tape recorder than he was in whatever activity I had arranged. The mud baths, hiking up Mt. Tamalpais, shooting pool, whatever. "I could do this on a regular basis," he said, sweating heavily after playing tennis with me near my home. That time he borrowed both a racquet and running shoes. Afterward, he kept his new pair of running shoes in the trunk of his car, just in case.

THE MEANING OF LIFE II

Have you ever lain back on a warm summer's night, looking up at the stars, and really wondered why you are here? What is your place in things, and what are you supposed to do with your life?

Yeah, well, neither have I.

Yet I ended up having a theory about Life, The Universe, and Everything—or at least the subset called "Life." You were introduced to this theory in the preface of this book. And since you've gotten this far, I might as well explain myself a little more.

My theory didn't come about while staring up at the stars, immersed in wonder over the immenseness of it all on a clear night. It came about while I was preparing for a speech. When you become well known for one thing, people just assume you can be trusted to generate brilliant insight into unrelated bodies of knowledge that have been mystifying humankind for millions of years. And they want you to share those insights before a herd of perfect strangers.

No, it doesn't make much sense. I got into Linux because I was a technology geek, not because I was any good at public appearances, let alone philosophizing without prudent limits. But few things in life make all that much sense, so I'm not complaining.

Back to the subject at hand.

This time I was invited to a local event in Berkeley called "Webrush." Normally I wouldn't even consider it, but the invitation came through the Finnish Consulate here in the United States and being a patriotic person (or at least feeling slightly guilty about hating snow and having moved abroad), I had stupidly said "Okay. *Jag gör det.*"*

Now, nobody expected me to talk about the meaning of life, least of all myself. But this event was about life in the networked society, and I was there as the Internet person and representative of Finland. Finland, due to Nokia (the largest, best, and most beautiful company in the world as any Finn will tell you), is into communications in a big way, and "the networked society" is where it is at. We've already discussed how there are more cell phones than people in Finland, and the current research into finding ways of implanting the things surgically at birth.

So there I sit, wondering what I should talk about regarding communications. Oh, I forgot to mention that most of the rest of the panel would be comprised of philosophers talking about technology. This is Berkeley, after all. The two things they take very seriously in Berkeley are Berkeley politics and Berkeley philosophers.

So what the heck. If they were going to have philosophers talking about technology, why not have a technologist like me talking about philosophy? Nobody should accuse me of not having balls. They might call me terminally stupid (and hey, they probably do)—but *chicken?*

Not this geek.

So there I am, feverishly trying to come up with a subject to speak about the next day. (I never get around to doing speeches until it is way too late, so late the evening before the event is usually when you'll find me worrying about it.) And I'm struggling there, trying to ponder the "communication society" and what it's all about, and what Nokia and all the other communications companies will eventually evolve into.

And the best I can do is to just explain the meaning of life.

It's actually not much of a "meaning." It's more a law of life, hereafter to be called "Linus's Law." It's equivalent to the second

*"Yes, sure, I'll do it."

law of thermodynamics in physics, but rather than explaining the devolution of order in the universe, it is about the evolution of life.

I'm not talking "evolution" in the Darwinian sense here. That's a different thing—for Webrush I was more interested in how society evolves, and how we moved from the industrial society into a communications society: What's next, and why? I wanted to make it sound good, and to make enough sense to convince an audience for the duration of a panel discussion. Everybody has his or her own agenda, and that day mine was to emerge alive from a panel discussion with two notable philosophers.

So why do societies evolve? What's the driving factor? Is it really technology that drives society?—which seems to be a common view. Was it really the invention of the steam engine that got Europe started as the industrial society, and eventually evolved us through Nokia and cell phones into the communications society? That seemed to be the philosophers' take on this all, and they seemed to be interested in how technology changes society.

And I, as a technologist, know that technology drives nothing. It is society that changes technology, not the other way around. Technology just sets the boundaries for what we can do, and how cheaply we can do it.

Technology, like the devices it creates, is at least so far inherently stupid. It's only interesting insofar as what you can *do* with it, and the driving force behind it is thus really human needs and interests. We don't communicate more these days because we have the means to do so—we communicate more these days because people are blabbermouths, and they *want* to communicate; and if the means aren't there, they will be created. Thus Nokia.

So, my argument went, in order to understand the evolution of society, you have to understand what really motivates people. Is it money? Is it success? Is it sex? What *fundamentally* makes people do what they do?

The one obvious motivational factor that probably nobody will argue with is simple: survival. That is what defines life, after all—it survives. It *doesn't* just blindly follow the second law of thermodynamics, but instead survives despite a universe that seems fairly inimical to the kind of complexity and order that is the very underpinning of life. So survival is motivational factor #1.

In order to rank the other motivational factors, I had to consider how they would stack up against that very simple will to survive. The question is not "Would you kill for money?" but "Would you *die* for money?" The answer there is clearly no. So we can safely strike money off the list of fundamental motivational factors.

But there are obviously things that people are willing to die for. There are a lot of heroic stories of people and even animals who are in fact willing to die for some larger cause. So plain survival alone does not explain the motivational factors that drive our society.

The other motivations I came up with for the talk in Berkeley were simple and not very contested at the panel. So at least somebody agrees with them. (Or, in consideration of the Finnish consulate, they were just being polite.) There aren't very many things that man is willing to die for, but social relations is definitely one of them.

The examples of social motivation being enough to drive people to forget about survival are numerous, from the literary Romeo and Juliet (dead not because they wanted anything as crass as *sex,* but because they would rather die than lose their social relationship) to the case of the patriotic soldier willing to risk his life for his country and his family—his society. So chalk up "social relations" as motivational factor #2.

The third and final motivational factor is "entertainment." That may sound trite, but it's unquestionably a very strong force. People die every day doing things that they're only doing for fun. Jumping out of perfectly operational airplanes just to get the rush, for example.

And entertainment doesn't have to be trite. It can be a game of chess, or the intellectual entertainment of trying to figure out how the world really works. It can be the curiosity and exploration of a new world. Anything that makes a person sit in a crowded rocket on top of a gadzillion pounds of highly explosive material just to be able to see the earth from space can certainly be called "motivational."

And that's it: *Survival. Your place in the social order.* And *entertainment.* The three things that make us do the things we do. Everything else is what a sociologist would probably call "emergent behavior"—patterns of behavior that emerge from those much simpler rules.

But it's more than just "these are the things that motivate people." If that were all, it wouldn't be much of a theory of life. What makes it interesting is that the three motivational factors have an intrinsic order, an order that shows up wherever there is life. It's not just that *we're* motivated by those three things—they also hold true for forms of life other than human life, and they show up as the natural progression for any lifelike behavior.

Survive. Socialize. Have fun. That's the progression. And that's also why we chose "Just for Fun" as the title of this book. Because everything we ever do seems to eventually end up being for our own entertainment—at least if we have been given the possibility to progress far enough.

You don't believe me?

Look at how we classify animals as "lower" or "higher" order animals. They all survive. But the higher you get in the evolutionary scale, the more you are likely to first create social patterns— even ants, fairly low down on the scale, have very strict social patterns—that eventually progress into having fun. Playing with your food is not something ants tend to do a lot. . . . But cats do. Ants don't enjoy sex, either.

Yes, take something as basic (and delightful) as sex. I don't claim that it is one of the fundamental motivational factors per se—but it's a great example of rather fundamental human behavior that has undergone the whole evolution of life. There's no question that it started out as a pure survival trait. After all, even plants have "sex" in the survival sense, and at some stage billions of years ago, sex was probably purely a survival thing for those single-celled animals that would slowly evolve into geeks and other humans. And there's no question that sex long ago evolved from a purely survival phenomenon into a very social phenomenon. It's not only among humans that you find marriage ceremonies and a lot of social infrastructure for getting laid. Think of the ritual dance of the Sandhill crane—which mates for life, by the way. In fact, inordinate amounts of energy get spent every day on the social courtship rituals associated with the simple matter of reproduction of all the species.

Entertainment? That too, I assure you. Not just among humans, but it is probably no coincidence that the most evolved species on the planet also seems to make the most out of the entertainment aspect of sex.

The progression of survival to social behavior to entertainment is everywhere. Take war: very much a survival trait back when the only way to get to the watering hole was to kill the people in your way who wanted that source of water for themselves. War has long since become a tool for maintaining social order in society. And with the advent of CNN, it has become entertainment. Like it or not, this seems to be the inevitable progression.

Civilization itself follows the same larger pattern. Originally it was a way to ensure survival by cooperation and power in numbers. That is nothing unique to humans. Most animals and even plant life create societies in order to survive better by helping each other. And what is so interesting is how society itself moves from being survival-based toward being more social; how all human civilizations end up building bigger and better roads and communication channels in order to be able to better socialize.

And in the end civilization too becomes geared toward entertainment. Look at the Roman Empire—famous not only for its road building and strong social order, but also, especially later, even more famous for its entertainment.

Or look at the United States today. Does anybody doubt that the film and computer-game industries are not about ushering in the entertainment society? From having been niche markets not that long ago, they are now among the biggest industries in the richest country in the world.

And what is interesting to me as a technologist is how this pattern repeats itself in the technology we create. We call the early age of modern technology the Industrial Age, but what it really should be called is the Age of Technological Survival. Technology, up until not that long ago, was almost exclusively for surviving better—being able to weave cloth better and to move goods around faster. That was some of the original impetus for it all.

We call the current period the Information Age. It's a big shift. It's about technology being used for communication and spreading information—a very social behavior—rather than just surviving in better style. The Internet, and the fact that so much of our technology is starting to move toward it, is a big road-sign of our times: It means that people in the industrialized countries are starting to take the survival thing for granted, and suddenly the next phase of technology becomes the big and exciting one: the social aspect of communication technology, of using technology not just to live better but as an integral part of social life.

The ultimate goal, of course, is still looming. Past the information society, the entertainment society. A place where the Internet and wireless communications twenty-four hours a day is taken for granted and doesn't get any headlines anymore. A time when Cisco is the old market, and Disney Corporation owns the world. A time probably not too far in the future.

So what does this all mean? Probably not much. After all, my theory of the meaning of life doesn't actually *guide* you in what you should be doing. At most, it says "Yes, you can fight it, but in the end the ultimate goal of life is to have fun."

It does, to some degree, explain why people are willing and eager to work on projects like Linux on the Internet. For me, and for many other people, Linux has been a way to scratch *two* motivational itches at the same time. Taking survival for granted, Linux has instead brought people both the entertainment of an intellectual challenge and the social motivations associated with being part of creating it all. We may not have seen each other face-to-face very much, but email was much more than just a dry exchange of information. Bonds of friendship and other social ties can form over email.

This probably also means that if and when we ever meet another intelligent life form in this universe, their first words are *not* likely to be "Take me to our leader." They're more likely to say "Party on, dude!"

Of course, I might be wrong.

Index

Morfar. *See* Törnqvist, Leo
  Waldernar
motivation
  influencing factors, xviii-xxii,
    244-49
  for programmers, 122, 227,
    228
Motorola, 41
Mozart, Wolfgang Amadeus,
  211
Mozilla (Netscape project), 155-
  57, 231-32
Mozilla Crypto Group, 157
MP3 technology, 216
multitasking, by computers, 41
music industry, recording technology and, 216-17

Napoleon, 13
Napster, 216
National Aeronautics and Space
  Administration (NASA), 161
Nesson, Charles, 226
NetBSD, 57
Netherlands Unix Users Group,
  113
Netscape, 20
  Mozilla project, 155-57, 231-32
networking, 117, 151
  Linux and, 116-17
newsgroups
  advocacy, 155-56, 157, 158,
    159, 162
  Linux, 117-18
Newton, Isaac, 94, 228
Nokia, 33, 94, 243, 244
Norssen High School (Helsinki),
  24, 25

Norway, 32
Novell, Inc., 57, 130

OpenBSD, 57
Open Law Project, 226
open source, 20, 114, 121-22,
  128, 141
  antiestablishment sentiment
    for, 161
  Apple Computer and, 149-50
  control issues, 218
  free software movement and,
    58, 166-67, 194-95
  future technology development
    and, 223-24
  General Public License and,
    58, 59, 96-97, 194-96,
    225
  IBM and, 157-58, 162
  idealist vs. pragmatist debate
    about, 163-66
  Informix and, 158-59
  intellectual property issues
    and, 204, 210, 230
  Netscape browser technology
    and, 155-57, 231-32
  Palm Computing and, 219
  programmer motivation and,
    122, 227, 228
  rationale for, 225-34
  Sun Microsystems and, 151,
    152
  See also Linux operating
    system
operating systems (OS), 75, 222-23
  early versions, 39, 41
  microkernel approach, 98-99,
    101, 104, 150

VA Linux, 135, 174-75, 177, 228
vector graphics, 46
VHS tapes, 217
VIC-20. *See* Commodore VIC-20 computer
Vierumaki, Jouko (Avuton), 49, 69, 72, 84, 94, 134, 239
Vikings, 13
Visor (computing device), 219
VMS operating system, 53, 55

Wendt, Ernst von (great-grandfather), 15
Windows NT operating system, 158, 160, 167
Windows operating system, 55, 118, 158
Wired (magazine), 153
wireless technology, 215, 248
    cell phones, 32-33, 243, 244
Wirzenius, Lars, 27, 58, 64, 108, 115, 127-28
Wosniak, Steve, 41

Wapit, 230-31
war, Torvalds's meaning of life theory and, xviii-xix, xxi, 247
Webrush (Berkeley event), 242-44
Web servers, Linux and, 157-58, 160, 226

X86 interpreter, 147
XENIX operating system, 108
X windowing system, 115-16

Zborowsky, Orest, 115-16